THE MISSING MESSIAH

TYNDALE
elevate™
ask. seek. find.

KYLE IDLEMAN
MARK E. MOORE

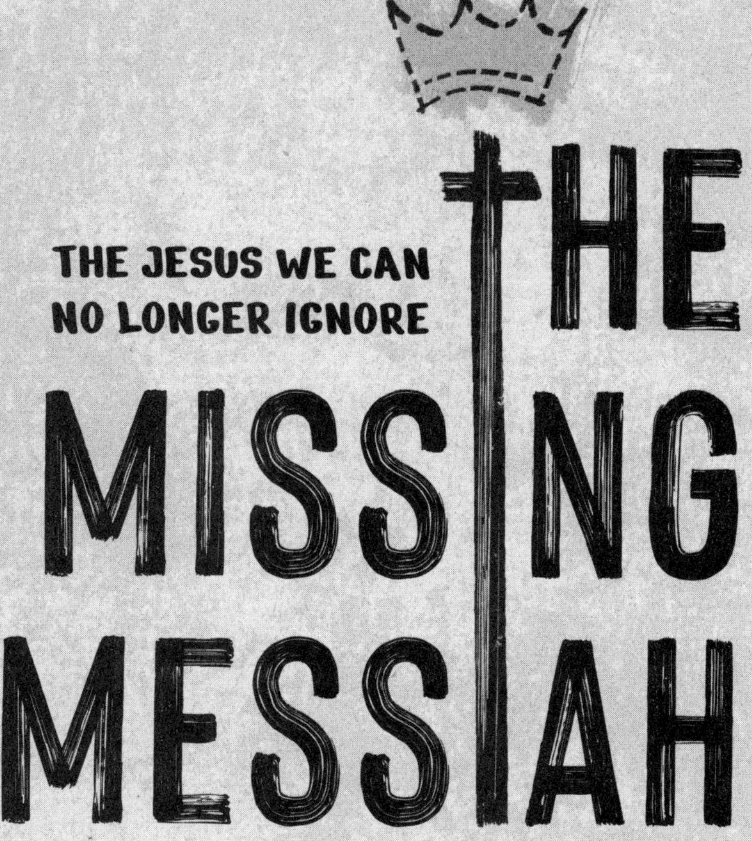

Visit Tyndale online at tyndale.com.

Visit the authors online at kyleidleman.com and markmoore.org.

Tyndale, Tyndale's quill logo, *Tyndale Elevate*, and the Tyndale Elevate logo are registered and/or common law trademarks of Tyndale House Ministries in the USA and various other jurisdictions around the world. All rights reserved. See tyndale.com for a full list of trademarks owned by Tyndale House Ministries. Tyndale Elevate is a nonfiction imprint of Tyndale House Publishers, Carol Stream, Illinois.

The Missing Messiah: The Jesus We Can No Longer Ignore

Interior design by Brandi Davis

Published in association with Don Gates of the literary agency The Gates Group; the-gates-group.com.

For information about special discounts for bulk purchases, please contact Tyndale House Publishers at csresponse@tyndale.com, or call 1-855-277-9400.

Library of Congress Cataloging-in-Publication Data
A catalog record for this book is available from the Library of Congress.

ISBN 979-8-4005-2517-9

Printed in the United States of America

32 31 30 29 28 27 26
7 6 5 4 3 2 1

CONTENTS

INTRODUCTION

WHERE IS THE MESSIAH?

When my son was in middle school, he pleaded for a pair of Air Jordan 4s. Not just any shoes—he wanted *the* Jordan 4s. He'd been dropping hints, showing me pictures on his phone, and finally he just came out with it: "Dad, I really need these shoes."

"Need?" I asked. "What do you need them for?"

"They're just . . . they're cool. Everyone's wearing them. They're classic."

Classic. That word caught my attention. So I asked him, "Do you know *why* they're classic?"

He shrugged. "They're Jordans."

"But do you know who Jordan is?"

"Yeah, Dad," he said with that tone teenage sons reserve for fathers who are obviously oblivious. "Michael Jordan. He was a basketball player."

To my son, Michael Jordan was just a logo. A brand. A name on a shoe that happened to be trendy. He had no idea about the flu game. The shrug. The last shot against Utah. Six championships. The way Jordan didn't just play basketball, he *transformed* it. Every other player became his supporting cast, whether they were his teammates or his opponents. He operated in a different dimension. My son didn't understand that Michael Jordan wasn't *a* basketball player; he was *the* basketball player.

To my son, *Jordan* meant style. To me, *Jordan* meant transformation.

Same name. Same shoes. Completely different meanings.

We've done something similar with Jesus. He has become our logo, our friend, our Savior, and our confidant who approves of us, forgives us, and encourages us. He does all those things, to be sure. But to reduce him to a brand borders on blasphemy.

Ask most people what *Christ* means, and they'll probably tell you it's Jesus' last name. As if Jesus had been born to Mary and Joseph Christ in Bethlehem and eventually started the religion that bears his family name. But *Christ* isn't a last name; it's a Greek title that means "Anointed One," or "Messiah" in Hebrew. Somewhere between the first century and today, we've forgotten what that title actually means.

When the first followers of Jesus called him *Christ* or *Messiah*, they were not giving him a surname; they were making an explosive political, theological, and revolutionary claim. They were saying that this carpenter from Nazareth was the promised King that Israel had been waiting for. The one who would establish God's Kingdom. The one who would challenge every earthly power. The one who deserves total allegiance.

In the first century, it was dangerous to call Jesus "the Christ." It was the kind of thing that got you killed. People didn't casually throw that title around. If you said someone was the Messiah, you were saying he was the rightful King, which meant Caesar wasn't. You were saying his Kingdom was ultimate, which meant Rome wasn't. You were pledging your allegiance to him above all other authorities.

That's what *Christ* meant.

But somewhere between the first century and the twenty-first, we've lost that meaning. We've turned a transformative title into a comfortable logo. We've turned the cross into jewelry or a trendy tattoo. We've domesticated a revolutionary claim into a religious label. And in the process, to some degree, we have lost *the Messiah himself.*

Oh, we still have Jesus. We talk about him constantly. We sing songs about him. We wear his name on T-shirts and put it on coffee mugs. We've built an entire religious-industrial complex around him, complete with a profitable marketing strategy. But the Jesus we have, the Jesus of modern Western Christianity, is neither the Messiah the first Christians knew nor the one his enemies feared.

We've created a personalized Savior who exists primarily to meet our individual needs, bless our lives, and guarantee our spots in heaven. We've made him into a spiritual life coach, a divine therapist, a cosmic vending machine who dispenses blessings when we pray the right prayers and live relatively decent lives.

That Jesus is safe. Manageable. Polite. Convenient. Eager to serve and save.

He validates our choices. He baptizes our politics. He asks very little of us beyond that we show up at church occasionally and are generally nice people. He fits comfortably into our lives without disrupting them too much. On Sunday mornings, we want just enough guilt to make us feel like we've been to church but not so much as to interfere with Saturday nights.

But here's the problem: That Jesus, the one we've made in our own image, would be unrecognizable to the people who followed him in the first century.

They didn't have a personal life coach. They had a King who demanded absolute allegiance.

They didn't have a spiritual therapist. They had a Messiah who told them to take up a cross and follow him, even to death. They didn't have a divine assistant who existed to improve their lives. They had a revolutionary who promised to turn the world upside down and who expected them to execute his mission—and, in some cases, be executed for the mission.

Same name. Completely different person.

It's like my son with the Jordan 4s. We've inherited the name. We've claimed the brand. We may have even made him a nostalgic hero. But somewhere along the way, we missed the story. We've lost what it truly means to call Jesus "the Messiah." We've lost the dangerous, demanding, glorious reality of who he is and what he came to do.

This book is about recovering that story.

It's about rediscovering the Jesus the original Christians knew, not just as Christ but as *the Messiah.* It's about understanding how Western culture has gradually reshaped Jesus into our image. It's about recognizing the difference between a personalized Savior and a revolutionary King. And it's about the high cost, as well as the greater gain, when we stop treating Jesus like a spiritual accessory and start following him as the infinite Messiah.

To be clear, this journey won't be easy. If you're looking for a book that reinforces your current understanding of Jesus, validates your lifestyle, and tells you that you're doing just fine, this isn't it. If you want a Jesus who fits neatly into your life without disrupting anything important, you're going to be disappointed.

But if you're willing to ask hard questions, if you're ready to discover that you might have been following a version of Jesus that is partial, shallow, or accessorized—an image Jesus wouldn't recognize in the mirror—if you're open to the possibility that there's a bigger, more dangerous, more majestic Messiah than the one you've inherited, then keep reading.

We didn't lose Jesus because he went somewhere. We lost him because we stopped looking for him. We settled for a smaller story, a safer Savior, a more convenient Christ.

But he's been there all along, waiting. Waiting for us to stop being satisfied with the logo and start seeking the living legend. Waiting for us to trade in our hand-me-down understanding of who he is for the real thing.

In the chapters ahead, we're going to trace how this happened, how the explosive title *Messiah* gradually lost its potent implications. We'll see what the first Christians believed about Jesus and why it got them killed. We'll discover what Jesus himself claimed about his identity and mission. And we'll wrestle with what it means to follow this Messiah in the twenty-first century.

This is going to challenge your assumptions. It might mess with your theology. It will definitely disrupt your comfortable Christianity. But it will also give you back the Jesus of the Gospels, the Messiah worth dying for, the King who demands everything, the Savior who doesn't just improve your life but completely transforms it.

The Messiah isn't missing, of course. We have been missing him. You are invited on this journey to chase hard after the Messiah and, along the way, make Jesus famous.

MOVEMENT 1

1

WHO DO YOU SAY JESUS IS?

"Daddy, can I put another heart in him?"

My six-year-old daughter stood at the stuffing station in the Build-A-Bear Workshop, eyes wide with wonder. We were celebrating her birthday, and she had chosen a fluffy brown bear that was now partially stuffed on the counter. The attendant smiled and handed her a small satin heart.

"Of course you can. The more love, the better!" At least, I'd like to remember responding with such supportive affirmation.

She remembers me using it as an opportunity to explain to her that bears only have one heart. Never mind the fact that it's not made of satin.

My daughter pressed the (second) heart to her lips, made a wish, and carefully tucked it inside her bear. Then the attendant helped her step on the pedal that would fill her creation with stuffing.

"How do you want your bear to feel? Super squishy or nice and firm?"

"Squishy!" my daughter declared without hesitation. "I want to be able to hug him really tight."

As the bear filled with stuffing, the attendant continued, "Now, what kind of voice do you want? We have growling or roaring, or you can record your own message."

My daughter chose to record herself saying, "I love you beary much!"

Then came the clothing options: princess dress, superhero outfit, sports jersey. She selected a rainbow tutu and a sparkly tiara. I put the football uniform back on the rack and reminded myself that this was her bear and she could customize it exactly how she wanted to.

As I swiped my credit card to pay for this personalized stuffed creation, it struck me that the Build-A-Bear was exactly the way she wanted it . . . but nothing like a real bear.

This isn't just a childhood teddy bear phenomenon; it's the air we breathe. We live in a culture obsessed with customization, where "Have it your way" has evolved from fast-food slogan to lifestyle manifesto. Our coffee orders have become paragraph-length recitations of personal preferences. Streaming services curate content with precise algorithms that are tailored to our viewing history. Our news feeds filter reality through the lens of our political leanings. Some of our medications even come with genetic testing to ensure optimal personalization.

From curated playlists to build-your-own burrito bowls, we instinctively assume the world should conform to our specifications. We're no longer just consumers; we've customized our consuming. The customer isn't just always right; the customer is now the designer, and the market scrambles to accommodate our every preference.

Personalization can be helpful. We're all unique, and it can be beneficial to find products and services that align with the way we're wired. But there can be a dark side to this, especially when it comes to spiritual truth. Somewhere between selecting our smartphone cases and personalizing our license plates, we've unintentionally found ourselves taking a "Build-A-Jesus" approach to our faith.

We decide how "squishy" our Jesus should be—firm enough to support us, but not so firm that he challenges our comfortable lifestyle. We select which voice we want him to have—perhaps he says, "I love you" or "You're forgiven," but certainly not, "Take up your cross" or "Sell your possessions." We dress him in accessories that fit our preferences—perhaps a pin matching our politics or a self-help book that promises prosperity.

This customized Jesus becomes a spiritual stuffed animal rather than a Messiah-King. We stuff him with attributes that make us feel secure—unconditional love, grace, and mercy—while conveniently leaving out his demands for justice, sacrifice, and surrender. We prefer the Jesus who rides on a donkey rather than the white horse described in Revelation. We choose the warm, gentle eyes of a Jesus who approves of our lifestyles, not the piercing gaze that saw through the religious hypocrisy of his day. We select the soft hands that heal and comfort, not the calloused hands of a carpenter who made tables and flipped them.

And so we end up dressing Jesus in whatever fits our aesthetics—conservative values, progressive causes, patriotic fervor, therapeutic spirituality—the list goes on. Just like my daughter's bear, our customized Jesus is designed primarily to make us feel good. He exists to comfort us, to assure us of heaven, and to be hugged tightly when we're scared, not to scare us with talk of repentance, sacrifice, or revolution.

This idea of a customized Jesus might sound innocuous. After all, shouldn't we have a Jesus who meets our needs—maybe one with two hearts? The danger is this (and it's a real danger): If we make Jesus in our own image, we're placing our hope in a false Messiah. If our Messiah is artificial, our hope is baseless and will fail under pressure. Our faith will be little more than a "Flat Stanley"—convenient for carrying in our pocket and taking selfies with, but not something we can build our lives on. The real Jesus is far more mysterious, dangerous, and exhilarating. Chasing after him is worth the risk—it will be the adventure of a lifetime.

HAVE IT YOUR WAY: THE CUSTOMIZATION OF CHRIST

I first realized how deeply I'd fallen into this "Build-A-Jesus" mentality during my third year as a pastor. I was preaching through the Sermon on the Mount, and as I prepared a message on loving our enemies, I found myself searching for ways to soften Jesus' radical commands. *Surely he didn't mean we should literally love those who harm us,* I thought. *There must be exceptions, qualifications, reasonable limits.*

That night, as I wrestled with the text, a disturbing realization washed over me: I wasn't trying to understand Jesus; I was trying to domesticate him. I was looking for loopholes because his actual teachings were too demanding, too disruptive to my comfortable worldview, too hard for people to hear. I wanted a Jesus who fit neatly into my upper-middle-class life, not one who would turn it upside down.

Christianity has largely been reduced to a transaction: Believe in Jesus + Improve yourself = Get to heaven.

This equation has become the dominant formula of modern faith. Getting into heaven is a transaction where the payment is simple intellectual assent, marked by repeating a prayer, walking down an aisle, or throwing up a hand.

While this idea is rooted in a powerful gospel promise, it's a reductionist view—one that threatens to diminish the revolutionary Messiah who overthrows empires into a passive savior who exists primarily to secure our afterlife. The Jesus who proclaimed, "The kingdom of God has come near" (Mark 1:15), has been relegated to a distant past and pushed to a distant future, his message stripped of its present power and urgency.

This cosmic transaction has become Christianity's primary selling point: Believe these doctrinal points about Jesus, and in exchange, you'll receive eternal life after death. Heaven has become the product, belief the price of admission. And in the process, we've reduced the Messiah to a mere ticket agent and his primary function to checking our ticket to make sure we can get through heaven's gates.

I've seen this firsthand in the churches I've attended and served. Our evangelistic approach can sometimes be summed up as "Are you going to heaven when you die?" The entirety of faith is compressed into ensuring our eternal destination. Week after week, the invitation at the end of the service is the same: "If you were to die tonight, do you know where you'd spend eternity?" The urgency is all about what happens after death, with almost no mention of how Jesus' Kingdom might transform our lives today.

But what if Jesus isn't just offering an eternal destination? What if he's inviting us into eternal life that begins now—a movement so radical that it will transform how we live, love, and lead today? What if the most dangerous misunderstanding about Jesus isn't found in secular culture but within our churches? We've mastered getting people ready for heaven while neglecting Jesus' invitation to bring heaven to earth. We've become experts at helping people die well while failing to show them how to live well in the Kingdom Jesus inaugurated.

When Jesus taught his followers to pray, "Your kingdom come, your will be done, on earth as it is in heaven" (Matthew 6:10), he wasn't offering a pleasant liturgical phrase; he was articulating the heartbeat of his mission. Yet we've sanitized this revolutionary prayer into a religious recitation while continuing to push God's Kingdom safely into the afterlife.

Is it possible that in our efforts to make Jesus accessible, we've made him unrecognizable?

The transaction-based gospel offers a Jesus who makes minimal demands in the present while promising maximum rewards in the future. It presents a Jesus who saves souls but leaves societies, systems, and daily lives largely unaltered.

Outside the University of Louisville, in Louisville, Kentucky, our church took a team to gather college students for a focus group. Participants were asked to give their gut response, without overthinking, to this question: "What features or attributes would you want in your ideal spiritual leader?"

The answers came quickly:

"Someone who helps me find my purpose."
"Someone who can get me into heaven."
"A comforter who reduces my anxiety."
"A guide who helps me figure out my life."
"Someone who supports my political views."
"A figure who gives me hope but doesn't demand too much."
"I'd want him to meet my needs, not make demands."
"Someone who's understanding when I mess up and doesn't make me feel guilty."
"I want spiritual guidance without all the religious rules."
"A mentor who helps me become my best self."
"Someone who makes me feel special and chosen."
"A leader who focuses on love and acceptance, not judgment."
"A spiritual figure who helps me achieve balance and success in my life."

Notice what's missing from these responses. The students didn't want a spiritual leader who points them to a kingdom and a higher standard. They weren't looking for a faith that demands allegiance, surrender, obedience, or sacrifice. These students didn't want a king; they wanted a consultant. They weren't seeking a Lord; they desired a life coach. And can we blame them? This is precisely the Jesus who has been marketed to them—the Jesus of the cosmic transaction, who exists primarily to meet their needs and secure their afterlife, not to command their devotion or transform their world.

We've turned Jesus into a product. Listen to popular sermons, and you'll hear how Jesus wants you to be happier, healthier, and wealthier. Pick up a bestselling Christian book and discover how Jesus can fix your marriage, advance your career, or ease your anxiety. And while it's true that Jesus cares about our relationships and our well-being, he came for a much greater purpose.

The transactional gospel has produced a transactional Jesus—one who offers heavenly benefits with minimal earthly disruption. We've placed him in our shopping cart along with our other lifestyle choices and personal preferences. We've accepted his offer of eternal life someday—and his role as our personal cheerleader, life coach, therapist, political ally, and success guru while we wait.

THE MESSIAH MISCONCEPTION

Jesus himself defined eternal life not as a destination but a relationship: "Now this is eternal life: that they know you, the only true God, and Jesus Christ, whom you have sent" (John 17:3). Eternal life isn't what we get when we get to heaven; it's what we get when we get Jesus.

Picture this: If someone proposed to you and gave you an engagement ring, and you said yes, but then you both agreed, "Let's not see or talk to each other until we get married in two years," that would be ludicrous. The ring isn't just a promise of a future ceremony; it's an invitation into a present relationship. Yet somehow, we've reduced following Jesus to securing our spot at the wedding, completely ignoring the relationship he's inviting us into today.

This redefinition of eternal life hit me like a thunderbolt when I was in seminary. I'd spent my entire Christian life thinking of eternal life as something that started after death—a future reward for present belief. But Jesus defines it as a quality of knowing, a depth of relationship that begins now. This means that eternal life isn't just about living forever; it's also about living now, in the reality of God's eternal Kingdom. It means knowing and understanding who Jesus claimed to be.

When Jesus asked his disciples, "Who do you say I am?" (Matthew 16:15), he wasn't conducting a theological pop quiz or determining his identity by taking a poll. He was asking the most consequential question any human can answer. Peter's response—"You are the Messiah, the Son of the living God" (Matthew 16:16)—wasn't just correct; it was revolutionary.

The Hebrew word *Messiah* (or *Christ* in Greek) carried explosive expectations in Jesus' day. It didn't simply mean "savior" in some vague spiritual sense. It referred to the promised King, the Deliverer who would establish God's reign on earth. The title was so politically charged that claiming it could get you executed, which, of course, is exactly what happened to Jesus.

Yet we've domesticated this revolutionary title. My guess is that most people today think that "Christ" is Jesus' last name rather than a declaration of his Kingdom authority. We sing about Jesus Christ without considering what his messiahship means for how we live today. In short, we've separated Jesus the Savior (who gets us to heaven) from Jesus the King (who demands our allegiance now).

It's important to understand that this division would have been incomprehensible to Jesus' early followers. For them, salvation wasn't merely about the afterlife—it was about being rescued from all that opposes God's rule and being brought into his Kingdom in the present. Jesus put it this way: "The kingdom of God has come near" (Mark 1:15).

HITCHHIKING VERSUS HIJACKING

History is littered with examples of how we've distorted Jesus to fit our agendas. The Crusaders marched under his banner while slaughtering those who didn't share their faith. In 1095, Pope Urban II launched the First Crusade with these words: "God wills it!" Thousands took up arms, stitched crosses to their garments, and proceeded to massacre Muslims, Jews, and even Eastern Christians in their quest to reclaim the Holy Land. Jesus said, "Love your enemies" (Matthew 5:44), and told Peter, "Put your sword away!" (John 18:11). Instead, Jesus was made into a warlord.

Later, American slave traders quoted Scripture to justify human bondage. They took passages like Ephesians 6:5 ("Slaves, obey your earthly masters") out of their intended context while ignoring the revolutionary equality proclaimed in Galatians 3:28 ("There is neither Jew nor Gentile, neither slave nor free"). Slave owners created a Jesus who supported their self-serving economic system rather than the Jesus who came to set the captives free (see Luke 4:18-21).

It doesn't get much more twisted than Nazi Germany. The Jewish Messiah was made into an Aryan executioner, exterminating his own countrymen. Nazi leaders removed the Old Testament from their Bibles and edited the New Testament to eliminate

Jewish references.[1] The Jesus who was born of Jewish lineage, who taught in synagogues, and who fulfilled Jewish prophecies was whitewashed into a Gentile champion of German nationalist ideology.

During the Cold War, American Christianity often portrayed Jesus as the ultimate anti-communist. The risen Lord who transcended all political systems became the mascot for free-market capitalism and national exceptionalism. The Jesus who warned about the dangers of wealth became the champion of financial success.

Today's prosperity preachers transform the man who had nowhere to lay his head (see Luke 9:58) into a champion of wealth accumulation. They promise that faith in Jesus will bring financial blessing, conveniently overlooking his warnings about money and his call to sacrificial living. The Jesus who told the rich young ruler to sell all his possessions (see Matthew 19:21) becomes the Jesus who wants everyone to become a millionaire.

It's easy to identify these misrepresentations in history. It's far harder to recognize the blind spots in our own thinking. Could our comfortable, personalized versions of Jesus be just as unrecognizable to the real Jesus as the sword-wielding Crusaders' interpretation of Christ? Are we any less guilty of reshaping Jesus to fit our cultural moment and personal preferences than those we so easily critique from the safety of historical distance?

I'm as guilty of this as anyone. In high school, I wore a WWJD ("What Would Jesus Do?") bracelet while carefully avoiding certain people who didn't follow Jesus and who lived in a way that was opposite of what I thought the Bible taught. I claimed to follow Jesus while avoiding the very people he would have sought out. I had created a Jesus who affirmed my comfort zone rather than challenged it. I can neither confirm nor deny, but I may have punched a kid in the face during a soccer match for using the Lord's name in vain. (Okay, that did happen.)

We create a "convenient Jesus," who fits neatly into our Sunday mornings but doesn't intrude on our Monday meetings. We compartmentalize our faith, keeping Jesus in the sanctuary while our business practices, entertainment choices, and financial decisions remain largely untouched by his teachings.

We imagine a "safe Jesus," who never offends anyone. In our desire to be winsome and relevant, we filter out his more challenging statements. We highlight his love but downplay his calls for repentance. We celebrate his inclusivity while ignoring his exclusive claims. This Jesus is acceptable at dinner parties and workplace conversations because he's been scrubbed of anything controversial.

We craft a "spiritual but not religious Jesus," who offers the wisdom of Yoda but makes no demands for committed community. This Jesus encourages personal prayer and meditation but doesn't insist that we gather with other believers, submit to spiritual authority, or participate in ancient practices like Communion and baptism.

We construct a "partisan Jesus," who conveniently agrees with our political platform. On the right, he becomes a flag-waving nationalist focused primarily on traditional family values and individual liberties. On the left, he transforms into a social justice warrior concerned exclusively with systemic change and collective action.

We mold a "middle-class Jesus," who blesses our pursuit of comfort and security. Our bloated homes are blessings from God, not idols that could be holding us back from abundant life. This Jesus wants us to have nice homes in safe neighborhoods with well-funded retirement accounts. He encourages responsible financial planning but never questions whether our resources could be better used for Kingdom purposes. His calls for sacrificial generosity are interpreted as suggestions for occasional charity, not a radical reorientation of our relationship with possessions.

We sculpt a "success-oriented Jesus," who measures ministry effectiveness the same way corporations measure quarterly earnings. This Jesus cares about numbers, growth, and influence. He wants bigger churches, larger platforms, and more efficient systems. The metrics of the Kingdom—faithfulness, service, and love—are replaced by attendance figures, social media followers, and fundraising totals.

We develop a "therapeutic Jesus," who exists primarily to heal our emotional wounds and boost our self-esteem. This Jesus is always affirming, never confronting. He wants us to forgive ourselves before seeking forgiveness from others. His primary concern is our happiness, not our holiness. He calls us to self-care more frequently than self-denial.

The revolutionary Messiah who flipped tables in the Temple, who challenged the religious and political powers of his day, who demanded complete allegiance from his followers, and who called for a radical reordering of values and priorities—this Jesus is far more challenging than the customized versions we create. And it's precisely this Jesus we need to rediscover.

THE COST OF CUSTOMIZATION

If eternal life starts with knowing God through Jesus, then misunderstanding Jesus has consequences far beyond theological debate. It affects how we live now. When we reshape Jesus into a spiritual life coach, political ally, or success guru, we miss the revolutionary King who offers something far greater than personal comfort or heavenly fire insurance.

I felt this tension acutely when I began pastoring in an affluent suburb in Southern California. Many in my congregation were successful professionals who wanted Jesus to bless their already comfortable lives rather than disrupt them. When I preached about Jesus' radical teachings on wealth, status, and power, I could feel the resistance. One businessman told me after a sermon, "I appreciate your passion, but we need to be realistic about how Jesus' teachings apply in today's world." What he meant was "I want a Jesus who fits into my lifestyle, not one who challenges it." (I may or may not have punched him in the face. Okay, that didn't happen.)

The Jesus of the Bible doesn't just invite people to believe certain things about him—he is recruiting for a revolution. His Kingdom isn't just coming someday; it is breaking into the present, challenging every system and structure that opposes God's rule. His call isn't to simple belief but to radical commitment.

Consider how he described discipleship: "Whoever wants to be my disciple must deny themselves and take up their cross daily and follow me" (Luke 9:23). These aren't the words of someone offering a comfortable religious experience or an add-on to our already established lifestyles. These are the words of a revolutionary King calling for complete allegiance.

For many of us, the danger isn't that we'll reject Jesus outright. It's that we'll accept a version of him that doesn't challenge us, change us, or call us into his revolutionary movement. We'll keep our "Build-A-Jesus"—the one who is comforting and comfortable—while the real Jesus stands at the door knocking, waiting to lead us into something far greater than religious consumerism. He is not a spiritual stuffed bear; he is a roaring lion on mission.

A REVOLUTIONARY DECISION

So here's the question: Are you willing to meet the real Jesus even if he doesn't match the version you've created? The comfortable Christ of Western Christianity bears little resemblance to the revolutionary Messiah who turned the world upside down. Are we prepared to abandon our cultural idol in allegiance to the King?

Take a moment to answer these questions honestly:

1. Does your Jesus exist primarily to get you to heaven or to establish God's Kingdom on earth through you?
2. Is your Jesus primarily concerned with your comfort and happiness or with your transformation and allegiance?
3. Does your Jesus reinforce your political and cultural values, or does he regularly challenge them?
4. Is your Jesus a comfortable addition to your lifestyle, or is he constantly disrupting it with Kingdom priorities?
5. Does your Jesus look suspiciously like you—sharing your preferences, prejudices, and perspectives—or does he transcend your cultural impressions?

6. Do you find yourself avoiding certain teachings of Jesus because they're too demanding or uncomfortable?
7. Is your relationship with Jesus primarily about what he can do for you or about what he wants to do through you?

In the pages ahead, we'll rediscover what *Messiah* meant in Jesus' world. We'll examine how the expectations for the Messiah developed through Scripture, how they were understood in Jesus' day, and how they challenge our domesticated gospel today. The most important question isn't who we want Jesus to be; it's who Jesus actually is—and whether we're ready to follow him as he truly is, not as we've reimagined him.

Jesus refuses to be our custom creation. There's a lot I don't know about Jesus. He is majestic and mysterious beyond the borders of my imagination. But this I know: He's claustrophobic. He will not be stuffed into the satin skin we've relegated him to. He *will* break out. He came as the Creator, the King, and the revolutionary Messiah, and the choice before us is clear: Will we settle for a transactional approach, or will we join the Messiah's movement that changes everything? Because the revolution Jesus started isn't finished. It's waiting for people who are bold enough to join it.

The real Jesus—the revolutionary Messiah—is waiting for us to put away our custom creations and follow him into the revolution he began.

2

CHRIST IS *NOT* JESUS' LAST NAME

It was our biggest fight ever, and it happened after thirty years of marriage. I wish I could say it was over something important, but it was trivial and, well, embarrassing. If you'd been in our kitchen that day, you would have thought we were acting out a comedy skit, but alas, we were both very serious.

It was about the dishwasher, specifically me loading it . . . Okay, it was about me *not* loading it. Usually, I'm pretty good about helping out around the house. I've always put my dishes in the dishwasher (my wife's memory may differ, which is why she's not allowed to edit this chapter).

Here's what happened. Every time I put dishes in the dishwasher, she would rearrange them. Every time! It felt like she was passive-aggressively giving me the middle finger (which she would *never* do). Nonetheless, over three decades, this minor irritation became a big burr in my saddle. So I passive-aggressively stopped putting any dishes in the dishwasher. I knew she would ask, which is why I prepared an undeniably clever answer. She asked. I answered, "If I'm too stupid to load the dishwasher correctly, I'll just let you do it."

As one might imagine, this did not have the desired effect. She replied, "You thought that was about you?"

It turns out she was a trained expert in loading the dishwasher to its maximum capacity. When she was growing up, the rule was that any dish that didn't fit into their dishwasher had to be washed by hand. She became a prodigy in the art and was merely exercising her gift.

It was not my proudest moment.

Nonetheless, I learned a valuable lesson: You can live with someone for decades and not fully know them because you write their story in your head rather than hearing it with your heart. We make some unsavory assumptions when we don't ask honestly or listen courteously.

Here's my question for you: Are you willing to assess how well you've inquired of Jesus and how intently you've listened to his answers?

Let's start with his title: Christ.

THE MEANING OF MESSIAH

The word *Christ* appears in the New Testament over five hundred times, always referring to Jesus. It's natural, I suppose, that we would associate it with his name, Jesus. However, it's a title, not a name. The Hebrew parallel to the title *Christ* is *Messiah*, and they both mean "Anointed One." We don't practice anointing in our culture, so it feels unfamiliar to us. For Jews, however, the act of anointing set someone apart for a specific role they were to assume. It was a rite of passage, like a graduation, a wedding, or a quinceañera. It marked a new role and responsibility in the community.

That raises the question: Who was anointed in the Bible? There aren't many people in this category. The first person Scripture records as being anointed was Aaron, the priest of Israel, and his sons afterward (see Leviticus 8:12-13, 30). Then there were the first kings of Israel—Saul, David, and Solomon—and the kings who followed them (see 1 Samuel 10:1; 16:13; 1 Kings 1:39). Finally, one prophet, Elisha, was anointed to succeed Elijah (see 1 Kings 19:16). So there you have it: priests, kings, and prophets. These were the primary leadership roles in Israel. The Messiah ("the Anointed One") fulfilled each of these roles.

That presents a problem for modern Western readers, since we don't have kings. (Well, the Brits have a royal family, but they're more like celebrities than figures who inspire reverence.) When Americans think of a king in a historical context, we remember the Revolution of 1776. When we think of a king in mythical terms, it conjures up figures from fairy tales.

I was reminded how unfamiliar the idea of royalty is to us when I visited our church's mission partners in Eswatini, one of the few remaining absolute monarchies in the world. One of our key stakeholders in the ministry is the minister of finance for the country. He is a devout believer who reports directly to the king. When he's called into the king's presence, he's expected to follow the ritual regalia. Even this minister of finance, a powerful political figure, has to get on his hands and knees to approach the king, never allowing his head to rise above the king's, which is especially difficult considering the official is over six feet tall. For a Westerner like me, this offered a jaw-dropping perspective. While the exact protocols for entering the king's presence are not the same in Eswatini as they were in ancient Israel, seeing this reverence for a king helped me realize how different my cultural assumptions are from those of the original audience of the Bible.

When we're called to Christ, we pledge allegiance to Jesus as King. That's clear in the New Testament. Yet because this whole idea of a king is so unfamiliar to us, we subconsciously dismiss it. The world of the Gospels is immensely different from ours, so much so that we often don't even register the differences.

This idea of a "missing Messiah" isn't a new problem. Mark begins his Gospel by saying, "The beginning of the good news about Jesus the Messiah, the Son of God." Notice that Mark uses two titles: Messiah and Son of God. *Messiah* would have resonated with his Jewish readers. But he was writing for Christians in Rome, the capital of the empire. *Son of God* was how the locals referred to their emperor. Both Jewish believers and Gentile converts would have a title for Jesus that reflected the highest ruler of their political systems.

On paper, *Son of God* (what Romans called their emperor) and *Messiah* (what Jews called their king) both describe the guy at the top, the ultimate authority in their respective worlds. But here's where it gets tricky: Just because two titles point to the same job description doesn't mean they have the same résumé.

When Greeks and Romans heard "Son of God," they pictured someone who was worthy of worship. When Jews heard "Messiah," they pictured someone who pointed all worship to Yahweh. An emperor could create his own rules. A Messiah would follow and enforce God's law. An emperor would rule over the tribes of Israel. A Messiah would restore them.

Same position. Completely different playbook.

As Mark states, Jesus is both the Son of God and the Messiah. But as time passed and the Jewish influence on the church waned, it became easier to redefine Christ through their the lens of culture. As the understanding of the Messiah as the fulfillment of prophecies faded in the early church, the idea of Jesus' kingship became easier to overlook.

The same thing happens today. Most English Bibles translate Mark 1:1 as "Jesus Christ" instead of "Jesus the Messiah." Only the New Living Translation and the New International Version use "Messiah"—and even the NIV didn't make that switch until 2011. After so many centuries of translation, it's easy to forget that the Messiah was a Jewish concept in the first place.

Here is the problem: When we adopt a word from another language, we naturally redefine it in ways that fit our understanding. Parents of teenagers run into this all the time, even when they're using the same language. "Jesus is rizzin'" doesn't mean to a teen what it does to grandma. Redefining foreign words inevitably means we miss much of the original meaning. We create our own stories and end up at an impasse in front of a dishwasher.

So, what would it look like to ask honestly and listen courteously? Let's examine what the Old Testament says about the Messiah and the kind of leader he would be. Fair warning: It's not as clear as we'd like. After all, these writers were predicting what was to come. March Madness, political cycles, and stock market predictions are just as unclear. Granted, the Old Testament sages had the advantage of inspiration from the Holy Spirit, but they were still seeing "in a mirror dimly" (1 Corinthians 13:12, ESV). The coming Messiah was as confusing for an Old Testament audience as the book of Revelation is for us, and for the same reason. It's like a weather forecast—we have predictions, not promises. The advantage we have (and we'll fully use this in the next chapter) is that we can see the Messiah in the rearview mirror, especially as Jesus described himself.

THE FACES OF THE MESSIAH

The Messiah, simply put, is the Anointed One, which conjures images of kings, priests, and prophets. Each of these titles for the Messiah has its own face, and each is embodied in a famous Old Testament figure. The king is, of course, David; the prophet is Moses; and the priest (surprisingly) is Melchizedek.

A King like David

Most messianic passages predict a royal figure modeled after King David (see appendix A). David's name appears thirty-two times in predictions about the coming Messiah. One of the most important predictions occurs during David's lifetime and comes from the prophet Nathan, who later confronted him regarding his sin against Bathsheba and Uriah. Nathan delivered God's promise to David (and ultimately about the Messiah): "When your days are over and you rest with your ancestors, I will raise up your offspring to succeed you, your own flesh and blood, and I will establish his kingdom" (2 Samuel 7:12).

This promise initially pointed to Solomon, who turned out to be a spiritual disappointment and whose successors divided the

Kingdom of Israel: "When he does wrong, I will punish him with a rod wielded by men, with floggings inflicted by human hands" (2 Samuel 7:14). Solomon, and those who followed him, couldn't fulfill God's promise. A Messiah-King was needed to correct the wrongs of previous kings. That's why verse 13 says, "I will establish the throne of his kingdom forever" (2 Samuel 7).

This Messiah-King is clearly depicted in Psalm 2. These verses, several of which are referenced in the New Testament, tell us three things about the Messiah-King: He would face opposition from his contemporaries (verses 1-2) but would be deeply loved by God (verse 7); therefore, we should be fearfully loyal to him (verses 11-12).[1]

This David-like King would be known for two main qualities. First, he would be a liberator of his people, and second, an annihilator of his enemies. As a liberator, he would be exceptionally good and kind to those he called his own. He would gather the lost tribes and bring them back to Israel after their long exile. When he freed the captives, he would bring liberty, light, joy, comfort, peace, and freedom. In this way, he was seen as the nation's Savior. This was the core of the Jewish expectations for the coming Messiah.

Yet there was another strand woven into the fabric of the Old Testament. The Messiah would also serve as a light to the Gentiles. This is clearly expressed in Isaiah 49:6, which says, "It is too small a thing for you to be my servant to restore the tribes of Jacob and bring back those of Israel I have kept. I will also make you a light for the Gentiles, that my salvation may reach to the ends of the earth." Somehow, this Messiah would be just as beneficial to the non-Jewish nations as he was to Israel.

This Messiah-King, exceedingly good, would also be terrible and terrifying to those who stand in opposition to his Kingdom. In fact, the very first prophecy about the Messiah promises a violent victory over his enemy, the serpent: "He will crush your head, and you will strike his heel" (Genesis 3:15).[2]

Here's where things get interesting. The Old Testament prophets spoke about the coming peace when the Messiah would arrive. But in the centuries between the Old and New Testaments—the gap between Malachi and Matthew—the Jewish writings started painting the Messiah as a warrior. Not just a King—a warlord.

What changed?

Pompey happened. In 63 BC, this Roman general marched into Jerusalem like he owned the place (which he kinda did). The violence and occupation that followed didn't just wound the Jewish people; it rewired their hopes. When you're getting beaten down, you start praying for someone who can beat back.

Violent rhetoric is almost always a response to violence experienced. The suffering we endure becomes the lens through which we see the world. That was true for first-century Jews waiting for their Messiah, and it's true for us today. What we're going through shapes what we're looking for in a Savior.[3]

A Prophet like Moses

In ancient Israel, a king could not be a priest, nor could a priest be a king. Since priests came from the tribe of Levi and kings came from the tribe of Judah, these two roles were mutually exclusive in Israel (similar to how the US government separates judicial, legislative, and executive powers). However, either a priest or a king could be a prophet. Both Jeremiah and Ezekiel were prophet-priests. Similarly, the first two kings, Saul and David, were kings who also prophesied (see 1 Samuel 19:23-24; Acts 2:29-30). Therefore, it's not surprising that the regal Messiah would be a prophet as well as a king.[4]

This Messiah-Prophet was, naturally, modeled after Moses, the founder of the nation: "The Lord your God will raise up for you a prophet like me from among you, from your fellow Israelites. You must listen to him" (Deuteronomy 18:15; see Acts 3:22-23). The Messiah, like Moses, would establish a renewed Kingdom, and like other prophets (such as Samuel, Nathan, and Elijah), he would promote righteousness, justice, and judgment.

He would teach truth, instill wisdom, and call for repentance. Isaiah captures it well: "The Spirit of the Lord will rest on him—the Spirit of wisdom and of understanding, the Spirit of counsel and of might, the Spirit of the knowledge and fear of the Lord. . . . With righteousness he will judge the needy, with justice he will give decisions for the poor of the earth" (Isaiah 11:2, 4).

One of the inevitable (and unfortunate) traits of prophets is that they often endured great suffering for challenging the authorities. They were, all too often, suffering servants of God. Yet even though a prophetic Messiah would have been standard fare to an Old Testament audience, a suffering Messiah would have seemed unimaginable. While the Old Testament alludes to a suffering Messiah three times, nowhere is that idea repeated in extrabiblical sources. Though rare and subtle, these three texts shed a little light on the idea of the Messiah as a suffering servant (see Psalm 118:22; Isaiah 52:13–53:12; and Zechariah 12:10). We will examine these in detail in chapter 8, but for now, suffice it to say that this small thread of prophecy becomes a major theme in the Gospels.

A Priest like Melchizedek

Kings came to Israel's political game a bit later, but priests were anointed leaders from the beginning. Since priests came from the tribe of Levi and kings from the tribe of Judah, these two roles were mutually exclusive in Israel. As noted earlier, a king could not be a priest, and a priest could not be a king. Yet the role of the Messiah included both roles. He would govern the political realm as well as the sacred space of the Temple, which in the new Kingdom would be his followers.[5] How can this puzzle be solved? The answer is to go back in time, before Israel had either a priest or a king. In fact, we go back as far as the patriarch Abraham. He paid a tithe to Melchizedek, the ruler of Salem, later Jerusalem (see Genesis 14:18-20). Melchizedek means "King of Righteousness," and he was a "priest of God Most High" (verse 18). Nothing else is known about his origin or genealogy. As a result, he became a mystical figure in both Jewish and Christian writings.

When the psalmist predicted a Messiah who was both royal and priestly (see Psalm 110), he drew on the imagery of Melchizedek. Melchizedek was a kingly figure, reigning over Zion with a throne next to God, a scepter in his hand, and an army at his command. He was also a priest. "The Lord has sworn and will not change his mind: 'You are a priest forever, in the order of Melchizedek'" (Psalm 110:4). Jesus used this same psalm to reveal his messianic identity to the Pharisees (see Matthew 22:44). Peter quoted the same psalm in his Pentecost sermon to show who Jesus was (see

Acts 2:34-35). Later, the writer of Hebrews used the same passage to talk about Jesus' priesthood (see Hebrews 5:6).

As the concept of the Messiah grows and develops through the latter part of the Old Testament, we hear more talk about a divine figure. Isaiah 9:6 declares: "To us a child is born, to us a son is given, and the government will be on his shoulders. And he will be called Wonderful Counselor, Mighty God, Everlasting Father, Prince of Peace."

This sparked a line of ideas that depicted a Messiah with divine powers. In Daniel 7:13-14, he is seated with Yahweh, worshiped by all nations, wielding God's authority as "a son of man." The inclusion of priesthood as part of the messianic role led the writers of the Old Testament to reference Melchizedek as a model, which in turn opened the door to some vivid, supernatural, almost fantastical images.

WHAT ARE WE MISSING?

Today, we don't have the same misconceptions as the early church did about the Messiah. We may not struggle to accept that he came to save both Jews and Gentiles. We may be able to embrace that he was supernatural but also that he had to suffer. We seem to have a good grasp on Jesus as the Savior of our souls. But we, too, are influenced by the cultural influences around us, and these contribute to our own blind spots about Jesus. Are we as clear about his lordship over our lives? What are we missing that the Old Testament audience and the early believers understood?

If we miss the Messiah-King, we will expect him to serve us rather than assuming we will serve him. If we miss the Messiah as Prophet, we may accept his past suffering but ignore his present call for us to carry a cross. If we miss the Messiah as Priest, we may see him more as a contemporary preacher than a Melchizedek who preceded Abraham himself.

It's natural to see Jesus as looking like the person in the mirror. The gravitational pull throughout church history is to remake him in our image rather than allowing him to reshape us into his. The risk of making him more recognizable is that we'll end up missing the fullness of who he is. We would be wise to take a fresh look, listen respectfully, lean in carefully, and humbly accept what Jesus said about his own role as the Messiah.

3

THE CHRIST CAPTCHA

Perhaps the most frustrating computer security tool known to humans is a captcha. It stands for "Completely Automatic Public Turing test to tell Computers and Humans Apart." (Even the name is irritating.) You've seen them. You get nine pictures, and you have to select each one that has a streetlight, a cat, or a bicycle. In other words, you need to distinguish "the thing" from "not the thing." Computers struggle with that. Honestly, so do I. Maybe the pictures are too grainy, the objects are too small, or I'm just too impatient, but these can be maddening!

They demonstrate that we're not as good as we think we are at seeing what's right in front of us. We tend to perceive what matches our expectations. Psychologists refer to this as *perceptual set.* Humans are conditioned to notice only certain things. Our contexts, cultures, and experiences influence this conditioning. Additionally, we naturally seek out evidence that confirms our ideas and desires. We tend to interpret information in ways that help us make sense of the world as we understand it or want it to be.

How good are you at noticing what's right in front of you? I'm sure you're above average. (I'm not—at least that's what my wife says.) But if you had to pick out all the aspects of the Messiah in a Bible captcha, would you be able to unlock the code? Could you distinguish the true images of Christ from the fakes to fully experience eternal life today, right here on earth?

Fortunately, we don't have to guess. Jesus provided us with all the insight needed to understand the true portrait of the Messiah. In fact, after his resurrection, Jesus explained his messianic role to the apostles: "'This is what I told you while I was still with you: Everything must be fulfilled that is written about me in the Law of Moses, the Prophets and the Psalms.' Then he opened their minds so they could understand the Scriptures" (Luke 24:44-45).

What did Jesus say about his role? What did he remind his followers of? In this chapter, we'll examine the main conversations Jesus had about his messianic mission. There are seven passages, like captcha images, that the New Testament uses to form the portrait of Jesus the Messiah.

CHRIST REVEALED TO THE SAMARITANS

One of the clearest descriptions of Jesus as the Messiah was revealed early in his ministry, and it came from his own lips. Traveling north through Samaria, he stopped at a historic well. It had been dug by Jacob, the father of the twelve tribes. Jesus sent his disciples into town to get supplies while he rested at the well, waiting for a woman. She had no idea who he was.

At that time, ethnic tensions between Samaritans and Jews

were volatile and violent, and interactions between men and women were carefully avoided. That's why, by the cultural standards of the time, Jesus should not have been talking to her, especially since she was probably considered scandalous by her community. Nevertheless, Jesus asked her for a drink.

Stunned, she replied, "You are a Jew and I am a Samaritan woman. How can you ask me for a drink?" (John 4:9). What Jesus said next was a spiritual depth charge: "If you knew the gift of God and who it is that asks you for a drink, you would have asked him and he would have given you living water" (verse 10). Gift of God? Living water? Her head was spinning.

This was Jacob's well. Jacob (also known as Israel) had dug that well to provide water for his family. His twelve sons became the patriarchs of the twelve tribes. Jesus was claiming to be greater than Jacob, offering "living water." In Jewish culture, *living water* referred to a flowing stream rather than a stagnant well. But it's more profound than that. Jesus says in John 4:14 that this water would bring eternal life, forever quenching all thirst. Given this bold claim, maybe we should capitalize "Gift of God" (verse 10). This gift is a person, not a thing.

Likewise, a case could be made to capitalize both "Spirit" and "Truth" in verse 23: "A time is coming and has now come when the true worshipers will worship the Father in the *Spirit* and in *truth*, for they are the kind of worshipers the Father seeks" (emphasis added). John has already claimed that Jesus is "full of grace and truth" (John 1:14). It's only possible to properly worship God through him.

This bombshell was a bit overwhelming for the woman. She tried to deflect the discussion by saying, "I know the Messiah is coming—the one who is called Christ. When he comes, he will explain everything to us" (John 4:25, NLT). Jesus' response was a nuclear blast: "I AM the Messiah!" (John 4:26, NLT). To truly understand this depiction of Jesus, we need to pay attention to two subtle points. First, the Greek phrase "I AM" represents the Hebrew word *Yahweh*. That would have been blasphemy . . . if Jesus couldn't back it up.

The second subtlety is the parenthetical comment John adds in verse 25: "who is called Christ." Twice, John transliterates the Hebrew word *Messiah*, spelling it with Greek letters (see John 1:41). He is reminding his audience that *Messiah* is originally a Jewish term. This subtle inclusion of the transliteration of *Messiah* serves as a reminder, perhaps a warning, not to forget the Jewish roots and original implications of this title, the prophetic promise of the Anointed One.

Originally, the early church was exclusively Jewish. But John reminds us that Gentile inclusion was Jesus' original intention. Jesus' final command to "go into all the world" (Mark 16:15) fulfilled God's Old Testament promise to restore Israel, not merely by bringing back the borders of Israel but by expanding Israel's borders to include the entire world, thus fulfilling the original promise to Abraham to bless all nations (see Genesis 12:1-3; 18:18; 22:18; 26:4; 28:14). It began here, with this Samaritan woman.

She raced back to the village to tell her fellow villagers, "Come, see a man who told me everything I ever did. Could this be the Messiah?" (John 4:29). This was a mesmerizing invitation, given her colorful past. They came out in droves and begged Jesus to stay. He stayed for two more days. When he left, they declared, "We know that this man really is the Savior of the world" (verse 42). We tend to interpret "Savior of the world" through evangelical lenses. But for the Samaritans, it had a more secular meaning. "Savior of the world" was a title used to honor the emperor. These Samaritans, reflecting their own messianic hopes, were not talking about the cross but the crown. They seemed to hope that Jesus would be a regal warrior of liberation. Jesus didn't say anything like that, at least not during this particular encounter.

Are we so different? We want Jesus to make our lives better, or at least easier. Like the Samaritans in this story, we want him to represent us, not the "other." What if Jesus' blessing in your life isn't to bless you but to bless others through you? Would that make a difference in how you used your finances and resources or how you leveraged your education and assets? Perhaps one measure of how much of the Messiah we're missing is how many others we overlook.

Scripture: John 4:1-42
False Concept: The Messiah came to improve our lives.
Reality: The Messiah came to give us eternal life, providing living water that allows us to become a spring of life for others.

CHRIST REVEALED IN HIS HOMETOWN

The next revelation of Jesus' messianic plans was not on foreign soil—it was in his hometown synagogue in Nazareth. Jesus had been busy getting baptized by John and being tempted by the devil. He returned home as somewhat of a local hero. This kind of attention also stirred up some envy among the people. He was "the carpenter's son," and many were quick to remind him where he belonged (Matthew 13:55; see Luke 4:22).

Jesus was invited to preach to his family and friends in a humble house of worship he had attended weekly since childhood. He knew every knot in every wooden beam, every wrinkle in every elder's brow, every dream and every secret of both friends and foes. He began his message with a powerful statement: "The Spirit of the Lord is on me, because he has anointed me to proclaim good news to the poor. He has sent me to proclaim freedom for the prisoners and recovery of sight for the blind, to set the oppressed free, to proclaim the year of the Lord's favor" (Luke 4:18-19).

Jesus then rolled up the scroll, handed it back to the attendant in charge of the synagogue service, and sat down. (Sitting down didn't mean he was finished; it meant he was just getting started, taking the traditional posture of a rabbi.) We have no idea how long he spoke. The only part of the message recorded was a single sentence: "Today this scripture is fulfilled in your hearing" (Luke 4:21). Perhaps that's all he said. After all, it was enough to trigger an avalanche from the crowd. Some were taken by his words; others couldn't get past his past: "Isn't this Joseph's son?" (verse 22). And this likely would have had the added implication of being his "illegitimate" son.

There is a world of meaning packed into this short sermon. Jesus was claiming to be the Anointed One. But what kind of Anointed One? Well, this definitely included the role of a prophet, since he was preaching the good news of liberation. In verses 25-27, he went on to compare himself with the quintessential prophets Elijah and Elisha.

That would have been enough to raise people's eyebrows, if not their ire. But *how* he made the claim would have been astonishing to them. Jesus quoted two separate passages that day. He began reading in Isaiah 61:1-2 and then rolled the scroll back a few chapters to 58:6. While this may not be obvious to us today, the audience definitely would not have missed it as Jesus maneuvered the large scroll on the wooden table in front of him. Had Jesus been reading from a liturgical text assigned for that day, it would have been a single passage. Instead, he deliberately chose these passages and combined them to make a specific point: *I am the Anointed One who will set captives free.*

Isaiah 61 was a popular passage in Judaism at the time. Other writers used it to show that the powerful Messiah would defeat Israel's enemies through military strength.[1] Jesus seemed to focus on the poor who were mistreated by their own people rather than by foreign conquerors. Specifically, he promised "the year of the Lord's favor" (Luke 4:19), or *Jubilee*. This ancient command from God required the cancellation of all debts every fifty years. As far as we know, Jubilee was never fully implemented, but the hope it represented was very real to those living on the brink of poverty. Jesus promised a release and freedom that showed he was much more than a carpenter.

There is one other detail that is easily overlooked. When Jesus quoted Isaiah 61:2, he stopped short of the final phrase "and the day of vengeance of our God." It's not that Jesus didn't see himself as an eschatological judge. Indeed, he did (see Matthew 7:21-23; 13:40-43, 49-50; 16:27; 25:31-46; John 5:22-30). But it was too soon for that kind of talk in Nazareth. For now, the focus was on release and remission.

So often we want Jesus to free us from discomfort. That was never his primary agenda. He came to suffer and serve, and he calls us to follow his example. He is far more interested in freeing us *for* than freeing us *from*. He frees us for service, mission, compassion, and justice. The modern church often focuses on protecting our values, freedom, and interests. Jesus, however, only used his power for the sake of the powerless. Following the Messiah is not about finding freedom but brokering it for others. This is a radical perspective we too often miss.

Scripture: Luke 4:16-30
False Concept: The Messiah offers freedom from our current struggles.
Reality: The Messiah bids us to preach good news to the poor and disenfranchised, sacrificing our own freedom to liberate the oppressed.

CHRIST REVEALED TO JOHN THE BAPTIST

About halfway through Jesus' three-year ministry, tragedy struck. John the Baptist, Jesus' relative, friend, and forerunner, was thrown into prison. His crime? Speaking out against Herod's incestuous and corrupt marriage. Herod Antipas had gone to Rome to seek greater power and influence. En route, he stayed with his brother Philip, who had married Antipas's niece Herodias. During his visit, Herod and Herodias conspired to divorce their spouses and marry each other, thus becoming the power couple of the country.

Is it any wonder that John the Baptist railed against their personal indiscretion and political corruption? Is it any wonder that Herodias despised John the Baptist, plotting his execution? Is it any wonder that John, while he was a political prisoner of Herod, wanted to know if Jesus was, in fact, the Messiah? After all, hadn't Jesus cited Isaiah 61:1, promising to free captives? John, rotting away in a prison cell in a remote desert fortress, sent a delegation to Jesus, asking if his hopes had somehow been misplaced.

Jesus' response combined Isaiah 35:4-6 and 61:1: "Go back and report to John what you hear and see: The blind receive sight, the lame walk, those who have leprosy are cleansed, the deaf hear, the dead are raised, and the good news is proclaimed to the poor" (Matthew 11:4-5). Most of us miss two subtle changes Jesus made in this citation. First, he left out the part about releasing those in prison. That was kind of a big deal for John! His imprisonment was likely what prompted his question in the first place.

Second, Jesus added a promise not found in Isaiah 35 or 61—or anywhere else in Isaiah, for that matter: "The dead are raised." Jesus is promising John resurrection. If you can imagine yourself in John's cell for just a moment, you might sense what John experienced: "I'm not going to release you from prison, but I will raise you from the dead." That's a pungent "good news/bad news" scenario, for sure. Essentially, Jesus was saying, "John, your hopes are not misplaced, but they are too small. I'm more than you imagined."

Maybe he's saying that to you right now, reading this book. You are longing for a get-out-of-jail-free card, and he wants to give you abundant life. He's worthy of your hopes. But he's aiming to do something bigger than you've dreamed. Like John, we have trouble seeing past our limited cell. In Christ, however, there is no limitation that can hinder us, no opposition that can stop us, no execution that can silence us. Because he is more than we ever imagined, we can live limitless lives, regardless of our current location or situation.[2]

Scripture: Matthew 11:2-6
False Concept: The Messiah will rescue us from our immediate troubles and trials.
Reality: The Messiah will raise us from the dead—literally someday and spiritually today.

CHRIST REVEALED TO HIS APOSTLES

Peter's great confession is the granddaddy of them all. It took place near Caesarea Philippi, a place known for the pagan worship of Pan. In that same area was Dan, the northernmost city of ancient Israel. It was at Dan (an archaeological site even in Jesus' time) that Jeroboam, the first rebel king of Israel, set up a golden calf (see 1 Kings 12:28-30). Dan symbolized the rebellion of the ten northern tribes against Judah and represented the broken unity of God's people.

Here's the background of that tragedy: When Solomon's son Rehoboam took office, the people begged for a tax cut. Solomon's wealth had come from the backbreaking labor of the people. They pleaded for relief. Rehoboam's young advisers told him to be tough. They counseled the new king to say, "My little finger is thicker than my father's waist" (1 Kings 12:10). That's the typical bravado of foolish youth. His older advisers gave the opposite advice: "If today you will be a servant to these people and serve them and give them a favorable answer, they will always be your servants" (verse 7). But Rehoboam ignored the advice of the wise. And when he increased the people's taxes instead, the Israelites turned to another leader—Jeroboam—and ultimately another god—the golden calf in Dan. It was as if Jesus had to come to this same area—a place pregnant with misguided meaning—to remind his own leaders of what kind of King he would be. If his disciples were to truly understand Jesus' agenda, they had to remember when and where their nation had failed.

In the place where the golden calf was installed, Jesus started the conversation by asking about public opinion: "Who do people say the Son of Man is?" (Matthew 16:13). The responses varied, but they all centered on human prophets who had been persecuted for speaking truth to power: John the Baptist, Elijah, and Jeremiah. The trajectory of Jesus' ministry was transparent. If Jesus kept preaching like these past prophets, his future would end up where theirs had. Of course, the Twelve couldn't imagine a suffering Messiah, and it was precisely this Messiah Peter was about to miss.

Jesus turned to the disciples and asked, "Who do you say I am?" (Matthew 16:15).

That's when Peter stepped up with an unusually insightful answer: "You are the Messiah, the Son of the living God" (verse 16).

Jesus affirmed Peter's response, emphasizing that it had to have come from God rather than from this ordinary fisherman. It was so good, in fact, that Jesus said he would build his church on Peter (and/or his confession) and that even the gates of hell would not prevail against it (see Matthew 16:18).

If Jesus were to ask you the same question, "Who do you say I am?" you'd likely get it right, for the most part. But are you, like Peter, missing the whole picture of who the Messiah is? Is it possible that you're missing part of his agenda and that what you're missing might put you at odds with where Jesus wants to take you? Anyone who trusts in Jesus as the Messiah will be truly free—free from sin and free for service. Recognizing the real Jesus fully—and developing a relationship with him—is the core of eternal life (see John 17:3).

Scripture: Matthew 16:13-20
False Concept: The Messiah is just a prophet and a great moral teacher.
Reality: The Messiah is fully human and fully divine, and his greatest work was to die for his enemies, not conquer them.

CHRIST REVEALED TO THE PUBLIC

Winter in Jerusalem can be cold. At around 2,500 feet above sea level, the windchill is often intense. It was winter when Jesus showed up at the Feast of Dedication, teaching on the cold stones of the Temple. In Solomon's Colonnade, he found some cover from the chill but none from the curious crowd plying him with questions. "How long will you keep us in suspense? If you are the Messiah, tell us plainly" (John 10:24). Jesus had often been cryptic about his messianic claims.

Though Jesus was clear with the Twelve, he told them to keep his identity quiet (see Matthew 16:20). Likewise, he silenced the demons when they began to out him as the Messiah (see Luke 4:41). The only other person he was open with was the woman at the well during their one-on-one conversation. Though the villagers there acknowledged him as the Messiah, news from Samaria would not have made headlines in Jerusalem.

Jesus would eventually claim to be the Messiah in Jerusalem (see Mark 14:61-62), but he hadn't yet. Meanwhile, every bread crumb he offered was rejected. Several months earlier, in that very city, in that very Temple, the crowds were arguing, "We know where this man is from; when the Messiah comes, no one will know where he is from" (John 7:27). Jesus tried to help them see his true identity: "Yes, you know me, and you know where I am from. I am not here on my own authority, but he who sent me is true" (verse 28).

This sparked a lengthy debate. Some people considered him a prophet, while others claimed he was the Christ (see John 7:40-41). They even raised a question about the prophecies concerning the Messiah: "How can the Messiah come from Galilee? Does not Scripture say that the Messiah will come from David's descendants and from Bethlehem, the town where David lived?" (verses 41-42). You're probably thinking, *But he was born in Bethlehem!* Yes, he was. But they didn't know that.

This little hullabaloo caught the attention of the Pharisees, the experts in Jewish texts. They were outraged that Jesus made claims bordering on blasphemy, such as, "I am the bread of life" (John 6:35) and "I am the light of the world" (John 8:12). Without using the word *Messiah*, Jesus sparked a heated debate, which ultimately led to the claim that ignited the religious leaders' ire: "'Very truly I tell you,' Jesus answered, 'before Abraham was born, I am!'" (verse 58). By using the very name for Yahweh (I Am), Jesus was asserting his preeminence over Abraham. That's when they tried to stone him.

So, at Solomon's Colonnade, Jesus was justified when he said, "I did tell you, but you do not believe" (John 10:25). He had just claimed to be the Good Shepherd who lays down his life for his sheep (see John 10:14-18). What else could that be referring to but the Messiah? After all, the image of a shepherd was one of the major metaphors for the Messiah (see Ezekiel 34:23-24; Micah 5:2-4; Zechariah 13:7). Given the volatile political context around the Messiah, is it any wonder that Jesus first proved his role through his actions before making overt claims?

That's exactly what he did and that's why he responded to the people at Solomon's Colonnade by saying, "I did tell you, but you do not believe. The works I do in my Father's name testify about me, but you do not believe because you are not my sheep" (John 10:25-26). Jesus' messianic claims were more than words. They were actions. His miracles, fulfillment of prophecies, sinless life, and divine insights in his teaching all proved he was the Messiah. He was *doing* messianic things, not just making messianic claims.

The very people who were looking for a Messiah missed him because he didn't show up in the way they expected. This begs the question: What might you be overlooking that causes you to miss the Messiah? What assumptions have you made about him that are influenced more by the world around you or your own preferences than the true picture painted for us in Scripture?

Scripture: John 10:22-39
False Concept: The Messiah will fulfill the prophecies the way I see them or at least prioritize the passages I prioritize.
Reality: The Messiah is a Shepherd who lays down his life for his flock. He may not remove our suffering, but he will absorb it.

CHRIST REVEALED TO THE PHARISEES

It was Tuesday, the week of Jesus' crucifixion. The political rhetoric was intense. Jesus stood in the Temple at the center of the turmoil. If you'd been there when he was teaching, you would have felt the tension as some of the major religious factions of his day accosted him with questions. When their attempts to trap him failed, he asked them a question.

It shouldn't have been a difficult one to answer. After all, Psalm 110:1 was a key prophecy about the Messiah. Jesus asked, "What do you think about the Messiah? Whose son is he?" (Matthew 22:42). They gave the correct answer: "The son of David." Then Jesus asked for an explanation of Psalm 110:1: "How is it then that David, speaking by the Spirit, calls him 'Lord'? For he says, 'The Lord said to my Lord: "Sit at my right hand until I put your enemies under your feet"'" (Matthew 22:43-44).

When you consider this question from the perspective of a Jewish leader from Jesus' day, you hear a conundrum. The first "Lord" is rendered in capital letters in Psalm 110:1 because it represents God's personal name, *Yahweh*. The second "Lord" is for *Adonai*, a title used for both God and people. So, Jesus said, how could David call the Messiah his Lord if he was his descendant? After all, in Jewish culture, the father was always seen as greater than the son.

The implication, of course, was that Jesus was the Son of God, not just the son of David. That was a conclusion the Pharisees dared not let see the light of day. So "no one could say a word in reply, and from that day on no one dared to ask him any more questions" (Matthew 22:46). It was such an effective argument, in fact, that Peter used the verse in his first public message on the day of Pentecost (see Acts 2:34-35), as did the writer of Hebrews (see Hebrews 1:13).

Now that Jesus was so close to his death, it was time to openly and publicly claim to be the Messiah—not just the son of David but the Son of God. His obedience through sacrifice and resurrection would demonstrate that he was God's Messiah.

The details may look different today, but our culture tends to make Jesus something less than the Son of God too. People may respect him as a moral teacher or a wise guru or someone who inspired hospitals and charity work. But people tend to squirm when we talk about him being the only way to the Father. Are there any ways that you may be toning down Jesus' divine nature, either because of your own discomfort or because of the views of those around you?

Scripture: Matthew 22:41-46
False Concept: The Messiah is an ordinary descendant of King David.
Reality: The Messiah is superior to King David, because he is also the Son of God.

CHRIST REVEALED TO THE HIGH PRIEST

During his trial before Caiaphas, the high priest, Jesus made his final messianic confession. Although Jesus was often cryptic in his public statements, his messianic actions were obvious enough. Rumors of his role had reached the highest levels of the religious hierarchy. Caiaphas, seeking a reason to execute him, pressed for a confession that could be labeled as blasphemy. It wasn't long in coming.

The high priest said to Jesus, "Are you the Messiah, the Son of the Blessed One?" (Mark 14:61).

"'I am,' said Jesus. 'And you will see the Son of Man sitting at the right hand of the Mighty One and coming on the clouds of heaven'" (verse 62).

Could Jesus have been bolder? Referencing Daniel 7:13, he claimed to be the heavenly figure at the right hand of the Ancient of Days, even using God's formal name, I Am. Jesus didn't cite the next verse, Daniel 7:14, but he hardly needed to, since it would have been well-known to a scholar like Caiaphas. That verse says that "authority, glory and sovereign power" were given to the Son of Man so that "all nations and peoples of every language worshiped him." You should have been there—Caiaphas blew a gasket.

The high priest tore his clothes and cried, "Blasphemy!" (see Mark 14:63-64). Jesus' destiny was determined not by Caiaphas but by the very prophetic utterances of God. The Son of Man fulfilled his role as the Son of God through suffering (see Hebrews 5:8-10). The idea that the Messiah would suffer seemed so outlandish that Jesus couldn't merely declare it with words. He had to demonstrate it with actions. Who else would conquer through suffering and lead by serving? Jesus was singular in the history of the world because he was not of this world. He came from the right hand of God, and there he returned, where he is now seated on his throne, ruling with divine majesty after suffering.

So often, we assume victory comes through strength—through powerful displays of bravado or shining success. Our Messiah, however, conquers in counterintuitive ways. He won through suffering. He brought life through his own death. He has the audacity to suggest that our greatest successes will follow his path of self-abnegation. The cross isn't merely something he did for us; it's the lifestyle he modeled for us as the path to greatness.

Scripture: Mark 14:53-65
False Concept: The Messiah is a powerful King who obliterates the opposition.
Reality: The Messiah is an eternal King who conquers through suffering.

CHRIST REVEALED TO YOU

It's easy to miss what's right in front of us. Unless we're explicit about what we're looking for, our expectations will filter out the unfamiliar, allowing us to reinforce our own biases. Jesus was clear, however, about who he is and what he came to do. Throughout his ministry, both through his actions and through his declarations about himself, Jesus defined *Messiah* for us in unmistakable terms.

It's time to tune out the white noise of our culture and the misconceptions about Jesus that have developed over the centuries. It's not that everyone is wrong. It's that Jesus alone can define for us who he is. That requires that we resist the gravitational pull of culture, habit, and our own desires so we can hear his voice above the noise.

4

MORPHING THE MESSIAH

My grandkids have a new favorite game called "Beat the Parents." It's really quite clever—the kids are asked a series of questions that parents normally wouldn't know. There are a lot of Pokémon and Minecraft questions that frankly sound like a foreign language to me. Similarly, the parents are asked questions that would befuddle kids, like the characters from *Friends* or *Seinfeld* or what in the world yellow pages are. My favorites are the ones about seventies rock, the greatest decade for music (feel free to argue with me on this point if you like to be wrong). The game isn't just fun; it's helpful because it allows family members to get to know each other across generations. If there can be such different life experiences, expectations, and vocabulary from one generation to the next, how much more so across two thousand years of church history? Perhaps we should lean in and listen more carefully to questions about the Messiah.

So let's back up and ask a simple question: Are Jesus Messiah and Jesus Christ the same thing? They used to be, during the early decades of Christianity. But as Christianity shifted from a Jewish sect to a global faith, it changed how Messiah was understood.

In Hebrew, *Messiah* (משיח, *Mashiakh*) means "Anointed One," just like the Greek word *Christ* (*χριστός*, *Christos*). However, having the same dictionary definition doesn't mean they had the same connotation in everyday life. They would have sounded very different to Jews and Gentiles. For Jews, the Messiah was a political figure who would rescue the nation from foreign oppression. For Gentiles (as we will see later), Christ became a title for Jesus the Savior—the one who rescues us spiritually, for eternity. As Gentiles came to outnumber Jews in the first-century church, it was only natural that the title *Christ* would overshadow *Messiah*.

Why does that transition matter to you as a modern Christ follower? We'll explore that throughout the chapter, but essentially, it matters because a title is more than a title, and a name is more than a name. It says a lot about our culture if we call someone a president, a prime minister, a king, or a dictator. Someone's role shapes our understanding of who they are and what we can expect them to do. Fair warning: We're going to dig a bit deep into history in this chapter. But if you hang in there, this will lay a foundation for the following chapters. More importantly, it will help us paint a more accurate 3D image of Jesus against the backdrop of his own worldview.

HOW THE IDEA OF THE MESSIAH MORPHED IN JUDAISM

Over fifteen hundred years, the Jewish concept of the Messiah underwent more transformations than a Hollywood diva.

Between the time of Israel's first king and the time of Jesus, this promised deliverer shifted in the cultural perception to include everything from a military leader to a political head, a cosmic judge to a divine messenger. The Messiah became whatever people desperately needed him to be, depending on the crisis they faced—whether it was cultural upheaval, historical calamity, or theological interpretations.

By the time Jesus arrived in the first century, Jewish expectations about the Messiah had become complex. Not every Jew expected the same kind of Savior, and some people weren't sure they needed one at all.

Four major moments in history had the biggest impact on shaping these messianic hopes: the failure of Israel's kings, the Maccabean revolt, Pompey's invasion, and the revolt against the Romans.

Seeking a Strongman

A thousand years before Jesus, Israel anointed its first king. Saul's reign ended in disaster. He failed so spectacularly that God ended his dynasty and chose David instead. The prophet Samuel delivered the bad news to King Saul: "You have not kept the command the LORD your God gave you; if you had, he would have established your kingdom over Israel for all time. But now your kingdom will not endure; the LORD has sought out a man after his own heart and appointed him ruler of his people" (1 Samuel 13:13-14).

David set the standard for what the Messiah should be. Although he wasn't perfect, he raised the bar for Israel's monarchy. But his mistakes still had consequences, and after his reign, everything rapidly went wrong. David's son Solomon broke every rule God had set for kings: Don't stockpile horses, don't marry multiple wives, and don't hoard silver and gold (see Deuteronomy 17:16-17). Solomon was the undisputed champion of each. It's not hard to see how his foolish son Rehoboam ended up plunging the nation into a devastating civil war because of his greedy tax policies.

This downward spiral led to disaster: Because of Israel's wickedness and idolatry, God allowed the Assyrians to conquer the ten northern tribes in 722 BC, and by 586 BC, the Babylonians had conquered the two southern tribes, destroying Solomon's Temple in the process. The nation was dispersed. The Holy City lay in ruins. Writings from this time period depict the coming Messiah as a strongman—someone who would reclaim the Promised Land by force.[1]

At first glance, we may think the idea of hanging our hopes on a savior who can conquer an enemy army is antiquated. But if we take an honest look at ourselves, how often do we find ourselves wishing God would take up our own causes instead of being consumed with *his* purposes? Jesus is indeed strong, but more often than not, he uses his strength to fight battles that aren't even on our radar.

Seeking a National Hero

Around 167 BC, a Syrian ruler by the name of Antiochus IV Epiphanes conquered Jerusalem. He was particularly brutal, determined to eradicate Judaism. He burst into Jerusalem, sacrificed a pig in their sacred space of worship (the ultimate insult), and began a campaign to kill any Jew who refused to worship his pagan gods. It was nothing short of genocide.

But in the small town of Modin, just northwest of Jerusalem, one priest—Mattathias—declared, "Not on my watch!" Instead of backing down, he fought back, killing the soldiers who were forcing his people into idol worship. What happened next became the stuff of legend—a fierce rebellion that, against insurmountable odds, somehow succeeded. The heroic deeds of Judas Maccabaeus (Mattathias's son) and his brothers read like a Marvel superhero origin story. They achieved the impossible: reclaiming Jerusalem and rededicating the Temple. This victory is still celebrated today during Hanukkah.

The Maccabean revolt completely changed how Jews viewed the Messiah, turning him into an apocalyptic hero. As the Jews' enemies grew more aggressive, their hopes for the Messiah intensified. But here's the tragic irony: The tremendous success of the Maccabean revolt led to the failed Hasmonaean dynasty. The descendants of those brave freedom fighters became the very kind of corrupt leaders they had originally fought against.

Through backstabbing and family feuds, the Hasmonaean princes drove the nation into complete political chaos. They ignored the rightful Davidic dynasty and instead spent their efforts on power-hungry scheming. Their greed plunged the nation into civil war, forcing them to invite outside help to settle their disputes. That "help" came from Roman general Pompey. His assistance, of course, came with strings attached—big ones. The price was losing their independence entirely.

The echoes of the Hasmonaean dynasty can be heard in the

halls of many modern churches. Religious leaders have used their positions and power to perpetuate their own agendas. The rise of the Western church has brought with it attempts to dominate those who disagree with our doctrines and social values. In many ways, success has been the greatest enemy of the church, because we have tried to use the power plays of the world to promote the Messiah. One of the sure signs that we're missing him is when our methods match the machinations of worldly rulers.

Seeking a Superhero

When Pompey marched into Jerusalem in 63 BC, it marked the end of an era. Jewish independence was over; Roman occupation was the new reality. Pompey brought his "peacekeeping" troops into the city and boldly marched into the Temple. He went straight into the Holy of Holies—the Temple's most sacred space—defiling it in the process. What he found inside was . . . nothing. The Ark of the Covenant was gone.[2]

To maintain control, Rome eventually installed its own puppet king—someone who had been raised in the ways of Rome. His name was Herod the Great. He was a political chameleon: Jewish when in Jerusalem, Roman everywhere else. His corrupt rule during the first century profoundly shaped messianic expectations. People were desperate for a legitimate Davidic Messiah to fix this mess.[3]

But that wasn't all they wanted. They realized they needed more than a national hero—they needed a larger-than-life superhero to solve problems bigger than any military could handle. They longed for a leader who could be both a "Messiah of Aaron" and a "Messiah of Israel"—a priest and a king, someone powerful enough to displace both the foreign-imposed King Herod and the illegitimate priests he had installed as his political puppets. They needed a supernatural figure to take the place of both. The language used to describe this figure—"just" and a "chosen one"—is the same terminology the New Testament uses to describe Jesus (see Acts 3:14; Luke 9:35).[4]

Centuries after Herod, we still face the same temptation to put human leaders on a pedestal, demanding that they use their power to support our "religious" agenda. This trend goes back to the early days of Israel, when the people clamored for an earthly king to protect them rather than trusting the living God. We demand that these leaders give lip service to our moral values even if they don't live them out. We elevate our idols above the Messiah. Consequently, we reshape Jesus into the image of our leaders rather than expecting our leaders to demonstrate the kind of justice and mercy exhibited by the Messiah.

Seeking Someone to Reinvent the Wheel

The Jewish revolt against Rome (AD 66–73) ended in catastrophe: the destruction of the Temple in AD 70. And here's the thing: It was never rebuilt. Without the Temple, sacrifices could no longer be performed. This forced both Jews and Jewish Christians to reinvent how they practiced their faith. Rabbinic Judaism emerged from the ashes of this crisis, shifting its focus to studying the Torah instead of making sacrifices at the Temple. Meanwhile, Christianity understood Jesus as the ultimate sacrifice and his church as the new temple. The destruction of the Temple didn't just change architecture—it triggered a complete reevaluation of what the Messiah was supposed to do.

What motivated the Jews to challenge the mighty Roman Empire in the first place? They were desperately hoping for a true Davidic Messiah who would defeat this Roman Goliath, and they were willing to die fighting Rome because they believed this Messiah was coming.[5]

But after the fall of Jerusalem, things got even more complicated. This revival of messianic fervor wasn't just caused by the loss of the Temple—it was also driven by the emerging Christian movement claiming that the Messiah had already arrived. Christians weren't focused on rebuilding the physical Temple; they were busy welcoming Gentiles as "living stones" in a new spiritual temple (1 Peter 2:5).

The catastrophe of AD 70 was pivotal to the way Christians perceived Jesus as the Messiah. Jesus had predicted this calamity with remarkable accuracy (see Matthew 24). Christians still believed, like non-Christian Jews, that the Messiah would eventually set things right and defeat his enemies, but the loss of the central place of worship emphasized that they now looked forward to this hope in the future—Jesus' second coming at the end of time. The destruction of Jerusalem's Temple shifted expectations about the Messiah from an immediate political idea to a more spiritual and universal idea, from freedom in the here and now to future redemption.

When the winds of culture shift, we often discover that the old way of doing things doesn't work anymore. The promises of the past seem like wishful thinking in the present. We may not let go of past promises, but we spiritualize them as metaphors. Miracles are seen as symbols or superstition. Carrying our cross is reduced to "mind over matter" thinking. Selling our possessions is code for tipping generously. Sharing our faith is about bumper stickers and screen savers.

Obviously, reevaluating our spiritual habits against our current reality can be healthy. But if we turn Jesus' commands into suggestions, his promises into aspirations, or his model into a metaphor, we're in danger of missing the Messiah.

HOW THE IDEA OF THE MESSIAH MORPHED IN CHRISTIANITY

The earliest Christian community in Jerusalem, led by the big three (James, Peter, and John), remained closely connected to Jewish practices and the Temple. Believers saw Jesus as the fulfillment of everything the Jews had been hoping for in a Messiah, although his suffering and death forced them to expand their playbook considerably. By the middle of the first century, when the Gospel writers started putting pen to paper, more and more non-Jews were joining the Jesus movement. Each Gospel writer provided a new perspective on Jesus the Messiah, helping readers understand him within their own cultural contexts. Their portrayals weren't contradictory—they were simply tailored to show how Jesus is relevant in different times and places.

The Messiah Through Jewish Eyes

Matthew and Mark both open their Gospels with an unprecedented claim: A real, flesh-and-blood person has fulfilled the messianic prophecies. This was groundbreaking. Matthew's version is deeply Jewish, going all the way back to Abraham: "This is the genealogy of Jesus the Messiah the son of David, the son of Abraham" (Matthew 1:1). He was born "king of the Jews" (Matthew 2:2), fulfilling Micah's prophecy about "a ruler who will shepherd my people Israel" (verse 6). Matthew showed how Jesus fulfilled—and exceeded—the traditional Jewish understanding of the Messiah. Through the account of the wise men from the East (verses 1-12), Matthew revealed how God's promise to Abraham was fulfilled through Jesus and demonstrated how that promise was not just for Jews but for Gentiles too, presenting a redefined Davidic Messiah who was marked by compassion rather than conquest.[6]

Mark took a different approach by crafting his introduction in language that would resonate with the Roman church: "The beginning of the good news about Jesus the Messiah, the Son of God" (Mark 1:1). Here's the thing: "Son of God" was a title usually reserved for the emperor. For a Jewish author living in the capital to apply it to Jesus showed serious guts. We see two different portrayals of the Messiah in just the first two Gospels, and we see a third in Luke's emphasis on Jesus as a prophet like Elijah (see Luke 9:8). Again, they're not contradictory—they're just tailored to their respective audiences.

John was the last to write his Gospel, probably around AD 90. By then, it was clear that these Greek and Hebrew terms (*Christ* and *Messiah*) carried different connotations. Twice, John wrote out the Hebrew word in Greek letters (*Messias*) and then translated it as "Christ" (*Christos*; see 1:41 and 4:25). This indicates that by the end of the first century, John's readers needed a reminder of the Hebrew roots of their Messiah. It could no longer be assumed that people understood the same meaning when they heard *Christ* as the first Christians did when they heard *Messiah*.

Each of the four Gospels presents Jesus in way that would have been culturally relevant to its respective readers. We need to do the same thing today, being aware of how our message about Jesus is interpreted by those who hear it. At the same time, the Gospel writers were vigilant to protect the words of Jesus and his self-revelation. Likewise, we need to be relevant without losing touch with the true identity of Jesus the Messiah. He is for all people, but he stands on his own terms. We morph to the Messiah rather than reshaping him to meet our needs.

The Messiah Through Greek Eyes

Here's an intriguing statistic: The Greek word *Christos* (*Christ*) appears 534 times in the New Testament, but only 10 percent of those instances are in the four Gospels. Jesus himself only used the term once publicly (see Matthew 23:10). Because of the volatile political climate of Roman-occupied Judea, Jesus claimed this title primarily through his actions (especially his death and resurrection) rather than through his words.

Around AD 50, under Paul's leadership, Jewish Christians launched an intense campaign to evangelize non-Jews. Gentiles generally knew little to nothing about Jewish Scripture or messianic expectations. Few spoke Hebrew, but nearly everyone spoke Greek. As a result, the Greek translation *Christos* was used for the Hebrew *Mashiakh*. *Christ* appears frequently in Paul's letters, functioning more like a proper name rather than a title.

Paul, as the apostle to the Gentiles, faced an enormous challenge. He needed to show Jesus as a powerful ruler who could stand toe-to-toe with Roman emperors while also revealing that Jesus represented a very different kind of leadership. This required careful cultural translation—and there were sure to be some misunderstandings along the way.

The political climate made things even more complicated. Julius Caesar was officially declared a god after his death, and his adopted son Octavian (later Augustus) was known as "son of god" (*dīvī fīlĭus*). When Paul referred to Jesus as the "Son of God" to Gentile audiences, the term carried unavoidable imperial connotations that required careful explanation.

Paul had to persuade Gentile converts that Christianity wasn't just another philosophy to debate in the marketplace of ideas but a life-changing relationship with the living God. He needed to shift their understanding of God away from a distant, mythical being who is indifferent to human affairs or morality.

As Christianity spread throughout the Greco-Roman world, it gradually adopted Greek philosophies and Roman organizational structures. This process, known as Hellenization, changed how Jesus was understood, interpreted, and portrayed. Greek philosophical ideas offered new frameworks for understanding Jesus' nature and his relationship with God. Terms like *logos* ("word"), used by John at the beginning of his Gospel, resonated with both Jewish wisdom traditions and Greek philosophical thought—an example of skillful cultural bridge building.

By the second century, Christian thinkers like Justin Martyr were explicitly applying Greek philosophical ideas to explain Christianity to educated Gentiles. Justin argued that Christ was the divine Logos (reason) in the flesh—a concept that would have resonated with Greek-educated audiences, even if Jewish messianic ideas confused them.[7]

As Christianity became predominantly Gentile, the understanding of *Christ* increasingly diverged from the Hebrew concept of *Messiah*. While linguistically equivalent, the terms began carrying different cultural, theological, and political baggage.

For Jewish Christians, *Messiah* remained linked to God's promises to Israel, the restoration of David's kingdom, and the establishment of God's rule on earth. For Gentile Christians, *Christ* increasingly became a proper name rather than a title, detached from its Jewish roots and reinterpreted through Greco-Roman cultural perspectives.

Whether we realize it or not, we are all products of the cultural air we breathe. Our political systems, educational systems, and family systems all create a lens through which we interpret the Bible. These filters aren't necessarily bad, but we need to be aware of them so we can recognize how they influence us. If they inadvertently obscure Jesus, we might be missing the Messiah without even knowing it.

The Messiah Through Philosophical Eyes

As Christianity spread like wildfire beyond the Roman Empire, theological ideas about Jesus became more sophisticated and complex. The development of Christology (the detailed study of Christ's nature and role) reflected both continuity with Jewish messianic hopes and major innovations influenced by Greek and Roman thinking.

The early church councils, starting with Nicaea in AD 325, began defining official doctrines about Christ's nature using Greek philosophical terms. Ideas like *homoousios* (meaning "of the same substance") to describe Christ's connection to God the Father would have been completely new to first-century Jewish Christians, but these words became essential to what is now recognized as orthodox Christian belief.

In the fifth century, the Council of Chalcedon (AD 451) established the mind-bending doctrine that Christ possessed two complete natures—fully divine and fully human—in one person. This formulation, while drawing on biblical texts, was expressed in categories borrowed from Greek philosophy rather than Jewish messianic thought. The understanding of the Messiah was undergoing a significant philosophical transformation.

The church fathers were trying to put words to the indescribable identity of Jesus the Messiah. God has given us his Word so we can understand his nature. He has also given us minds to help us put ideas about him into words. The reality, however, is that Jesus is far beyond what the human brain and earthly language can grasp. This calls for integrity and humility. Humility challenges us to admit that our perception of Jesus is limited and flawed. Integrity demands that we keep seeking the deep, authentic, and revealed nature of our Messiah.

The Messiah in Our Own Image

The rest of the story about Jesus as Messiah follows a familiar historical pattern. Christianity spread across the Roman Empire and ultimately became the official state religion under Emperor Theodosius I in AD 380. As the Western Roman Empire declined, the church stepped in to preserve classical learning and provide institutional stability—essentially becoming the glue that held civilization together.

The medieval period saw Christianity split into Eastern Orthodox and Western Catholic traditions, each developing its own distinct theological emphases and worship styles. The Reformation in the sixteenth century created further schisms in Western Christianity, resulting in a surge of Protestant denominations.

The Enlightenment arose and challenged traditional Christian authority, promoting rational ways of thinking about religion that made many long-held beliefs seem outdated. Colonial expansion spread Christianity worldwide but often in ways that were more influenced by European cultural assumptions than by the essentials of the gospel.

Within modern Christianity, you'll find a mind-boggling array of theological movements and church divisions: Catholicism, Orthodoxy, Protestantism, Calvinism, Pietism, Methodism, Pentecostalism, fundamentalism, evangelicalism, and postmodern Christianity.

While there's something to be said for finding a church that feels like home, a place where you can worship in a way that connects with you, there's a potential dark side to this. For one thing, it's easy to find ourselves in an echo chamber where everyone else thinks just like we do and where the Jesus portrayed agrees with us on every point. Another danger of staying in our separate corners is that it divides the universal church. But the greatest danger, in my opinion, is making Jesus our servant rather than us submitting ourselves to his service. The only way to capture Jesus' true image is to remain in God's Word and to hear about him from a wide variety of voices.

RECOVERING THE TRUE MESSIAH

Here's the bottom line: Many modern Christians understand a "Christ" shaped by centuries of interpretation, philosophical ideas, and cultural shifts. This Christ has been examined, debated, and broken down in many ways, often barely resembling the Messiah promised in Scripture.

Without realizing it, people have created their own personalized Jesus Christ, crafted to suit individual preferences and social beliefs. The problem? This customized Jesus may have little in common with Jesus the Messiah, the Son of God.

The shift from "Jesus Messiah" to "Jesus Christ" reminds us that all theology is shaped by culture—it's affected by the time and place where it develops. Understanding the original settings of biblical texts can dramatically enrich our grasp of their meaning. We must challenge our own cultural assumptions to see how they influence our view of Jesus.

If you want to truly understand your best friend, it helps to know something about their origin story—where they grew up, where they went to school, who their mentors and heroes are. If you want to know why certain things matter deeply to your spouse, you need to know the people and places integral to shaping who they are and what they value. In a similar way, the original Jewish context of Jesus' messianic identity remains essential to truly knowing who he was—and is.

5

WHEN JESUS GOT WEIRD

Weird might be hard to define, but you know it when you see it (often at family gatherings). And if you don't know any weird people . . . how do I say this gently . . . *you* are them.

TikTok is all the evidence you need to prove that people can be weird. Here are some of the top TikTok trends from this year: Lego pain tolerance tests (where you purposefully walk barefoot across a Lego-strewn floor and see how long you can handle it), human hamster challenges (where you spend the day spinning on a wheel and generally living like a hamster), reverse eating (which involves rewinding videos to ultimately reveal unchewed food), and underwater karaoke (which somehow involves singing while submerged).[1]

My guess is you don't need TikTok to tell you some people can be weird. The point of those examples isn't necessarily for you to record your own video but to tell you what you already know: People can be weird.

There's a different kind of "weird" that social scientists have identified—one that doesn't involve bizarre TikTok challenges. It's a weirdness so pervasive in our culture that we don't even recognize it as unusual. Like fish unaware of the water they swim in, we are immersed in a particular kind of cultural weirdness that shapes everything from how we think about ourselves to how we understand God.

HOW WESTERN INDIVIDUALISM RESHAPED OUR FAITH

In 2010, a team of social psychologists led by Joseph Henrich published a groundbreaking paper with an unusual title: "The Weirdest People in the World?" The researchers weren't referring to eccentric individuals or fringe subcultures. Instead, they were describing people who make up the vast majority of research subjects in psychological studies: people from Western, Educated, Industrialized, Rich, and Democratic societies—or WEIRD, for short.[2]

Each component of WEIRD culture shapes our faith in distinct ways:

- **W**estern philosophical assumptions prioritize individual reasoning over communal discernment;
- **e**ducation leads us to approach faith intellectually rather than as an embodied practice;
- **i**ndustrialization fragments our lives into specialized compartments, including a separate category for spiritual matters;
- **r**iches cause us to be self-dependent; and

- **d**emocracy conditions us to "vote" on the spiritual practices we prefer rather than submitting to spiritual authority.

WEIRD people in our Western culture have become the new normal. Our weirdness is seen in how we perceive the world, process information, make moral judgments, and understand ourselves in relation to God and others.

Maybe about now you think I'm weird for focusing so much on weird people. And you're wondering . . . What does this have to do with Jesus?

Everything.

The Jesus we've been taught about—the Jesus we pray to, worship, and invite into our lives—has been profoundly shaped by WEIRD cultural assumptions. The way we read Scripture, participate in church, understand evangelism, approach worship, and even conceptualize salvation are all seen through the WEIRD lens of our culture. While we may believe we're encountering the authentic Jesus of history, we're often meeting a Jesus who has been filtered through centuries of Western philosophical thought and, more recently, through the hyperpersonalized lens of modern individualism.

Don't get me wrong—I'm not saying this is a deliberate distortion. Have you ever worn sunglasses for so long that you forgot you had them on? You're looking around the house for them, trying to remember the last time you wore them; meanwhile, you've had them on the entire time. You're looking through the very thing you're looking for, so you don't notice them. You've worn them long enough that the tint has become the color of the world around you. We're looking at Jesus through WEIRD lenses, and we don't even realize it. For example, instead of seeing Christianity as a communal movement of the Messiah, we see it as a campaign for individual salvation and personal self-fulfillment.

Robert Putnam, in his book *Bowling Alone*, documents how American community life has been steadily declining since the mid-twentieth century. We've shifted from joining bowling leagues to bowling alone, from community engagement to individual consumption, from shared experiences to personalized entertainment feeds.[3]

Christianity in the West has followed this trajectory from community to customization. Even our language betrays this shift. We speak of "personal salvation," "my walk with the Lord," "private devotions," and "accepting Jesus as my personal Savior." We read the Bible alone in our "quiet time." We've reimagined faith as a primarily individual journey rather than participation in a revolutionary Kingdom.

I was sitting in a church service one Sunday when at the end of the message, the pastor instructed us to "close your eyes and imagine you're the only person in the room" before extending an invitation to "make a personal decision for Christ." I understood the intention, but as the saying goes, "What you win them with, you win them to." The pastor was inadvertently reinforcing the idea that faith is fundamentally a private, individual matter rather than entrance into a community with a shared story and mission.

THE GREAT WEIRD-ING: HOW WE GOT HERE

The WEIRD-ing of Jesus didn't happen overnight. It's the culmination of centuries of Western philosophical thought, accelerated by specific social and technological developments in the latter half of the twentieth century.

Western philosophy, from Plato to Descartes to Kant, gradually elevated individual reason and experience as the primary sources of knowledge and truth. The Protestant Reformation, while recovering important biblical truths, also had the unintended consequence of promoting individualism with its emphasis on personal Bible reading and direct access to God without institutional mediation. Again, these are not bad things—being able to read the Bible ourselves and knowing we can approach God directly are beautiful privileges that have nourished faith across generations. But along the way, we've gradually moved away from Christian community. It's like the slow drift of a ship that has lost its anchor. No single wave carried us out to the WEIRD Sea, but over the years, there has been a profound, if imperceptible, shift in our Western understanding of Christianity.

The Enlightenment further elevated individual reason, and American political philosophy enshrined individual rights as the cornerstone of society. While it was once inconceivable to sever Christianity from its communal roots, the pendulum has swung so far in the past few centuries that many Christians can hardly conceive of faith as anything other than a private, personal matter.

But if we want to identify a moment when American society took a WEIRD turn that significantly impacted our understanding of Jesus, we might look to the early 1960s. In 1960, G. D. Searle and Company's birth control pill received widespread FDA approval. While this resulted in some positive cultural shifts, including increased opportunities for women, it also contributed to a social revolution that fundamentally altered gender roles, family formation, and sexual ethics. A person's sexual life was increasingly viewed as a matter of personal preference, completely separated from social consequences.

At the same time, television was overtaking American homes, offering a more privatized entertainment experience. President Kennedy launched the space race, accelerating investment in scientific education and technological development. The postwar economic boom was creating unprecedented middle-class affluence, enabling more Americans to pursue individual consumption and leisure activities. While many of these developments weren't necessarily bad, each subtly normalized the idea of viewing everything through the lens of personal choice and individual fulfillment.

In the decades that followed, these trends only intensified. The self-esteem movement of the 1970s made personal feelings and self-perception central concerns. The consumer revolution of the 1980s elevated personal choice to nearly a fundamental right. The digital revolution of the 1990s and 2000s created ever more personalized media environments and social networks that sorted people by affinity rather than proximity. Today, algorithms have only gotten more sophisticated, and we're bombarded by content and advertisements that are all about us, all the time.

A number of years ago, my daughter's phone died, and she asked if she could use my phone. That seemed harmless enough, so I passed it over to her. I didn't know what she was doing, but it turned out she was shopping for a prom dress. How do I know? Because I was suddenly being assaulted with pop-up ads for prom dresses. For the next month, I couldn't check fantasy football scores without being offered a great deal on an evening gown. To this day, I know way too much about the styles and trends of prom dresses in the early 2020s.

Our customization culture is perhaps best illustrated by Netflix. When we log into Netflix, each of us sees a different streaming service. We're entering a personalized entertainment universe that revolves around our personal preferences. The customization begins the moment we first interact with the platform. Those initial selections set in motion a sophisticated algorithm that increasingly tailors our entire streaming experience to our individual desires.

The personalization goes far deeper than most viewers realize. The thumbnails you see for the same show differ from what other viewers see. For *Good Will Hunting*, some users see Matt Damon and Minnie Driver in a romantic embrace while others see Robin Williams in a dramatic moment. Even the categories themselves are algorithmically generated. While some broad groupings like "Action" or "Comedy" appear for everyone, there are thousands of hyperspecific micro-genres like "Scandinavian Romantic Dramas" or "Critically Acclaimed Fight-the-System Documentaries." I made those up, but you get the idea. And yes, there are a surprising number of Scandinavian romantic dramas, if that's what you're into.

This Netflixization extends far beyond entertainment. From news feeds to music services, from retail sites to search engines, our digital ecosystem constantly reinforces the belief that everything should be customized to our preferences, be served up according to what we like and, just as significantly, shield us from what we don't like.

Is it possible that, without even realizing it, we look at Jesus through this same lens? We've been trained by thousands of daily interactions to expect our world to conform to our preferences. We assume that content should be curated to match our established tastes and that experiences should be personalized to fit our individual profiles. Gradually, imperceptibly, we begin to approach Jesus as if he were a Netflix algorithm—highlighting the aspects of his teaching that align with our existing preferences, filtering out what challenges us, and reshaping his image to match the content we've already indicated we prefer.

The challenge for Christians in this Netflixized world is to consider whether we're treating Jesus as a personalized content provider rather than the uncompromising Lord who calls us beyond our preferences and into his universal Kingdom. For centuries, we've enjoyed a smorgasbord of denominations that suit our preferences. For decades, technology has given us the power to choose our personal brand of pastor, whether in person, on TV, or online. For years, Google has fed us the sites we wanted for Bible searches. Now AI knows more about you than you do.

The point is, our faith doesn't exist in isolation from these cultural shifts, and the way we see Jesus has been shaped in ways we don't recognize, or at least underestimate.

YOUR OWN PERSONAL JESUS

In 1989, Depeche Mode released the song "Personal Jesus." It became one of their biggest hits, and if you're over forty, you probably have the song playing in your head right now. I apologize in advance if it doesn't go away by tonight. If you aren't familiar with the song, the hook goes like this: "Your own personal Jesus / Someone to hear your prayers / Someone who cares." It perfectly captures the emerging spiritual ethos of late-twentieth-century Western culture.

While I appreciate the sentiment of those words, the song presents faith not as submission to the Messiah-King but as a personalized service relationship—Jesus as the ultimate personal assistant, available on demand to meet my individual needs. It's a Jesus who comes when called and exists primarily to serve me, kind of like a divine AI. This Jesus makes few demands beyond affirming personal authenticity. He exists primarily to comfort, guide, and support me on my self-determined life journey.

The sociologist Christian Smith has documented this drift toward our own personal Jesus in his research on "moralistic therapeutic deism."[4] He makes the case that this is the de facto religion of many people in the West. This belief system casts God as a cosmic therapist and divine butler who exists primarily to help us feel good about ourselves and solve our personal problems. Jesus is less the Lord who commands our allegiance and more the friend who supports our self-actualization.

It's no coincidence that this therapeutic, individualized Jesus is perfectly adapted to modern consumer capitalism. He demands nothing that would disrupt the way we spend our money, the way we use our time, the way we treat those we're in relationship with, and the way we engage with our communities. He focuses more on our personal well-being than on communal transformation. He fits neatly into our compartmentalized lives as one more resource for self-improvement.

Philosopher Byung-Chul Han observes in *The Burnout Society* that modern individualism has produced not liberation but a new form of self-exploitation. We have become "achievement-subjects" who are obsessed with continuously optimizing ourselves.[5] In this context, even Jesus can be co-opted as a means of self-actualization, a spiritual supplement to our wellness regimen rather than the revolutionary King who calls us to die to self for the sake of his Kingdom.

HOW WEIRD READING RESHAPES SCRIPTURE

Let's consider how WEIRD thinking has transformed core Christian practices like Bible reading.

Early Christians primarily encountered Scripture through public reading in community gatherings. The Bible was understood as the community's book, interpreted within the context of shared faith and practice. Individual copies of Scripture were rare, and the idea of interpreting the text based solely on personal perspective never would have crossed their minds.

Today, we primarily encounter Scripture through private "devotional" reading. We ask, "What does this verse mean to me?" which isn't a bad question but is certainly not the first or most significant question. Bible apps allow us to curate personalized reading plans and receive daily verses selected just for us. Even from the pulpit, some Scriptures are used to support a position rather than serving as the point of the message.

While there's certainly a place for allowing Scripture to speak to us and convict us in personal ways, this needs to be part of a broader understanding of God's Word as it applies to the church as a whole. In order to recover the biblical Jesus, we need to intentionally read Scripture through a less individualistic, more communal lens. Biblical scholar Richard Hays suggests we must learn to read the Bible with the eyes of the community rather than solely through individual interpretation.[6] This means engaging in conversation about Scripture with diverse believers, especially those from non-WEIRD cultural contexts, who might see what our individualism blinds us to.

A few years ago, my family and I spent a couple of months in Haiti, where we were helping some local Haitians start a new church. While we were there, I had long conversations with Edry, their pastor. One afternoon, we were sitting in the shade outside Edry's one-room home, a simple concrete structure with openings for windows and a tarp covering the doorway. His four children played nearby while his wife prepared a modest meal of rice and beans, somehow stretching the ingredients to feed their family plus an American visitor.

Edry sat across from me on a weathered plastic chair, wearing the same blue button-down shirt I'd seen him in for three days. Between us was a single well-worn Bible, its pages marked with notes, highlighted passages, and dog-eared corners. We had been discussing the Gospel of Luke, and Edry asked about my understanding of the parable of the rich fool in Luke 12.

"This parable," I confidently explained, "is about prioritizing spiritual wealth over material possessions. It's warning us not to be so caught up in our careers and material success that we neglect our relationship with God. It's about having the right perspective on wealth."

Edry listened patiently, his eyes kind but searching. When I finished, he was quiet for a moment.

"My brother," he finally said, placing his hand on the open Bible between us, "may I share how we understand this passage in our church?"

"Of course," I replied, genuinely curious.

"In our community, we do not see this parable as primarily about this man's personal perspective or priorities," Edry explained. "Jesus is speaking to a community where some have much and others have little. When the rich man says, 'I will tear down my barns and build bigger ones,' we hear this as a direct challenge to how wealth functions in community."

He pointed to the text: "Notice how many times the rich man says *I* and *my* in these few verses. My crops, my barns, my goods, my soul. But God calls him a fool. Why? Because he stored up treasures for himself but was not rich toward God. And how is one rich toward God? By being rich in community."

Edry gestured toward his children playing nearby. "When we read this in our church, we understand that building bigger barns while neighbors ache with hunger is foolishness. It is not about having a better perspective on your wealth while keeping it. It is about recognizing that excess grain has been entrusted to you to share with others. Your American reading makes this a parable about attitude. Our Haitian reading makes this a parable about action toward others."

I felt a slight defensive reaction rising. "But Jesus doesn't explicitly say the man should have shared with others. He's criticizing the man's self-focus, his greed."

"Yes," Edry nodded. "But in our culture, we understand that self-focus and failure to share are the same sin. When Jesus says, 'Life does not consist in an abundance of possessions,' we hear this not as a call to a better attitude about our possessions but as a call to hold possessions differently in community."

He continued, "When we read Scripture here, we always ask first, 'What does this mean for us?' not 'What does this mean for me?'"

I looked around at Edry's home—one room for six people, with almost no personal possessions. I thought about my own house back in America, my closet full of clothes, my personal study filled with books, many of them unread. I thought about how easily I had spiritualized this passage, making it about attitude rather than action, about perspective rather than practice.

"In your American context," Edry said gently, "perhaps it is easy to read Scripture as addressing only the heart because you have the luxury of choosing what to do with excess. Here, we read Scripture through the eyes of community because our survival depends on one another."

That conversation with Edry didn't just change how I understood one parable. It revealed how thoroughly my individualistic cultural lens had shaped my reading of Scripture. I had unconsciously reduced Jesus' radical economic teachings to matters of personal attitude rather than communal action. My WEIRD cultural assumptions had allowed me to feel spiritually mature while maintaining patterns of consumption and accumulation that the earliest Christians would have likely found incomprehensible.

THE UN-WEIRD-ING OF FAITH

If we want to adjust the lens through which we view Jesus, we must begin by becoming more conscious of how our culture influences our perception and shapes how we think about faith.

When Paul wrote, "Do not conform to the pattern of this world" (Romans 12:2), he was addressing believers embedded in the patterns of Roman imperial culture. Today, WEIRD patterns constitute the world we often unconsciously conform to. Paul continues, "Be transformed by the renewing of your mind." This renewal is an ongoing process, not a onetime action. When we submit ourselves to God's transforming work, he will enable us to see Jesus for who he really is.

The Jesus we meet in Scripture had a distinctly un-WEIRD cultural lens:

He was Middle Eastern, not Western.

He lived in an oral culture with limited literacy, not a highly educated society.

He was embedded in a collectivist culture that prioritized group identity over individual self-expression.

He lived in material simplicity, not affluence.

He existed under imperial rule, not democracy.

So it's not surprising that this Jesus announced a Kingdom, not merely personal salvation. His teaching addressed social relationships, economic practices, and political realities, not just private morality or individual spirituality.

Most significantly, this Jesus called his followers to surrender their individual identities to a new community formed around himself and to lose their lives so they could find them. His vision of human flourishing is not about self-actualization but about self-surrender for the sake of God's Kingdom.

So how might we begin to move beyond our WEIRD assumptions about Jesus and toward a more authentic encounter with the real Jesus, as revealed in Scripture? We will look together at a biblical perspective on Jesus and consider how our practices might shift to align with it. But as we do, please understand that these ideas aren't mutually exclusive—there's a valid place for both individual and communal practices. The key is to open our eyes to the ways our WEIRD lenses have led us to prioritize the former at the expense of the latter.

Here are five ways we can embrace a fuller, more accurate picture of Jesus.

Shift #1: From Personal Devotions to Communal Reading

Supplement private Bible reading with communal practices. Join a group that reads Scripture together. Find a church that prioritizes reading the Bible and treating it as the inspired Word of God. Seek out believers from different cultural and socioeconomic backgrounds to broaden your perspective on Scripture passages. Consider using ancient practices like *lectio divina* (the slow, meditative reading of Scripture) or responsive Scripture readings in a setting with others. Read commentaries from non-Western Christians to encounter perspectives shaped by different cultural assumptions.

Shift #2: From Individual Spirituality to Shared Practices

Embrace spiritual disciplines that can't be practiced alone. Consider inviting people into your home regularly for a meal (hospitality), volunteering at a food pantry or as a mentor to teens (service), forming an accountability group with trusted friends (confession), or seeking to heal a broken relationship (reconciliation). These practices help counterbalance our individualistic tendencies by embedding our faith in relationships.

Shift #3: From Consumer Worship to Participatory Gathering

Seek ways to contribute to a church service rather than merely being a receiver of it. This might mean joining a ministry team, participating in congregational responses, or simply approaching worship with the question "How can I love God and others?" rather than "What am I getting from this experience?"

Shift #4: From Personal Salvation to Kingdom Participation

Reframe your understanding of salvation to include not just individual forgiveness but also participation in God's redemptive work in the world. Jesus proclaimed, "The kingdom of God has come near. Repent and believe the good news!" (Mark 1:15). Jesus' message wasn't primarily about the destination of individuals after death but about God's reign breaking into the present. In this framework, salvation takes place not merely as a personal transaction but in the context of God's Kingdom and redemptive work.

Shift #5: From Digital Faith to Embodied Community

Recognize the limits of disembodied, digital spirituality. Online resources can supplement but not replace the embodied community of believers gathered in physical proximity. The church is not a virtual community but a flesh-and-blood reality. Of course, there may be times when, because of sickness or circumstances, we're not able to meet with other believers in person. But the default setting for church should be in a physical place, where you can read someone's body language, exchange a hug, hear the Word of God read aloud, see a need firsthand, and have in-person conversations.

Let me say it again for the people in the back: None of these shifts mean we abandon personal faith or minimize our individual relationship with Jesus. Rather, it means we recognize that authentic Christian faith, while always personal, is never private—it's inevitably embedded in community. It means we acknowledge that our individual perceptions of Jesus are shaped by cultural forces we often don't recognize.

When we take off our WEIRD lenses, the Jesus we encounter will likely be more challenging than our personalized version. He'll make demands we'd prefer to ignore, call us to forms of community we might find uncomfortable, and challenge cultural assumptions we take for granted.

This Jesus—the living, un-WEIRD Jesus of Scripture—doesn't exist to validate our individualistic lifestyles or affirm our personal preferences. And if you ask me, he almost certainly never made a TikTok video.

MOVEMENT 2

6

THE MESSIAH THEY PREDICTED

We've all been there: You're rushing through the airport, frantically patting your pockets for your ID. You wait in the (potentially eternal) security line so you can have your face scrutinized against your driver's license or passport. In this era of REAL IDs, proving who you are is not for the faint of heart. This wallet-sized card is equipped with holographic images and was created with specialized printing. To get one, you need a birth certificate, a Social Security card, proof of residency, a DNA sample from your liver, and, in some cases, a court order documenting your name change. Okay, the part about the liver sample isn't true, but it doesn't feel like that much of an exaggeration.

Why such intense scrutiny? Because in our AI age, where digital doppelgängers lurk around every corner, identity matters more than ever. The sobering truth is that when the stakes are high, casual identification simply isn't enough.

How much more important is it to confirm Jesus' identity as the true Messiah? Is he genuinely the Messiah foretold throughout the Old Testament? After all, it's not just physical safety that's at stake; we're talking about eternal security. Just as ID cards have specific, nonnegotiable criteria set by the government, there were clear, nonnegotiable traits outlined in Scripture for the Messiah.

PROVING JESUS IS THE CHRIST

If someone asked you to give Jesus a messianic TSA PreCheck, would you be confident you could screen him properly? Could you demonstrate, beyond question, that he is the real Messiah? The goal of this chapter is to give you the tools you need to do just that—and it might be more important than you realize.

All the "big boys" in the early church made a point of showing Jesus as the real Messiah. In Peter's first public sermon, his main goal was to prove that Jesus was the Messiah by demonstrating how he fulfilled the necessary conditions of Old Testament prophecy (see Acts 2:31, 36). Then came Saul (also known as Paul), the apostle to the Gentiles. While still dripping wet from baptism, he set out to prove that Jesus was the prophesied Messiah. He "baffled the Jews living in Damascus by proving that Jesus is the Messiah" (Acts 9:22). And let's not forget Apollos, who turned biblical prophecy into a master class in messianic validation. He "vigorously refuted his Jewish opponents in public debate, proving from the Scriptures that Jesus was the Messiah" (Acts 18:28).

Proving Jesus was the Messiah was not just a hobby for these church leaders; it was the focus of their preaching. Jesus himself showed them how to do this—he set the gold standard for this prophetic proof the very day he rose from the dead. He encountered two despondent disciples who were traveling to Emmaus. They were throwing in the towel because they thought Jesus was still wrapped in burial clothes.

Suddenly, this stranger sauntered up and, point by point, prophecy by prophecy, proved that the Messiah had to suffer. He rebuked them for their disbelief: "How foolish you are, and how slow to believe all that the prophets have spoken! Did not the Messiah have to suffer these things and then enter his glory?" (Luke 24:25-26). Wait . . . record scratch . . . the Messiah had to suffer? Had to die? This was the plot twist nobody saw coming!

A dead Messiah seemed like an oxymoron. Scriptures predicted that the Messiah would live forever (see Psalm 16:10). If the Messiah was dead, surely he couldn't be the real deal. No wonder those disciples were heading home with their hopes in their sandals.

To be fair, Jesus had been dropping breadcrumbs about his death throughout his ministry. He warned the disciples multiple times, and in specific detail. The first major clue came right after Peter's great confession—talk about emotional whiplash! One minute Peter was getting praised for recognizing Jesus as the Messiah, and the next minute Jesus was mapping out the path to his own crucifixion: "From that time on Jesus began to explain to his disciples that he must go to Jerusalem and suffer many things at the hands of the elders, the chief priests and the teachers of the law, and that he must be killed and on the third day be raised to life" (Matthew 16:21).

This was such a shock to their systems that Peter pulled Jesus aside and gave him a piece of his mind: "'Never, Lord!' he said. 'This shall never happen to you!'" (Matthew 16:22). The

Greek phrase, roughly translated, would be "No way!" or, in a fisherman's salty vocabulary, "H-E-double-hockey-sticks, *no*!" Messiahs didn't suffer; they definitely didn't die. Wasn't that precisely what Satan suggested to Jesus when he tempted him in the wilderness (see Matthew 4:1-11)? "You don't have to die. You can bypass the brutality of the cross." Because Peter was parroting the devil, Jesus rebuked him, saying, "Get behind me, Satan! You are a stumbling block to me; you do not have in mind the concerns of God, but merely human concerns" (Matthew 16:23).

Peter would have been right, if not for the resurrection. This surprising plot twist is the only way to justify a crucified Messiah. This singular event—the resurrection—is the turning point for all human history and the only lens through which a crucified Messiah makes sense. The resurrection is necessary because no one other than Jesus could fulfill the prophecies, and he did so down to the tiniest detail.

Chapter 9 will be dedicated to the resurrection, but for now, let's focus on the requirements for the Messiah. If we were to create a divine identity verification for the Messiah (think LinkedIn profile meets FBI background check), what would the nonnegotiables be? At the risk of oversimplification, here are the minimal prerequisites the Messiah had to meet:

- Family tree: He would be a descendant of David's royal bloodline.
- Birth: He must be born in Bethlehem, to a virgin (difficult to prove; even harder to pull off!).
- Job qualifications: He must perform miracles (not just party tricks—we're talking healing-the-blind-level stuff).

- Ethnic inclusion: He must be a light to the Gentiles (no hometown cliques allowed).
- Suffering servant: He must endure rejection, betrayal (specific price: thirty silver pieces), and crucifixion.
- Resurrection: He must rise from the dead and then ascend to heaven.
- Spiritual leadership: He must serve as both priest and king (think Melchizedek 2.0).
- Future orientation: He must establish a new covenant (not like a software update but an entirely new program).[1]

Jesus fulfilled all these prophecies about the Messiah—something that would have been statistically impossible on a human level. He might not have been what the people expected, but he was indeed what the Scriptures predicted.

This serves as a critical reminder for us too: When Jesus doesn't meet our expectations, we might want to revisit our biblical interpretation. God's Word never changes or fails, so our best bet is to measure our beliefs against the Bible and live according to it.

THE TIMELINE FOR THE SON OF GOD

The Old Testament predicted a Messiah who would be a king like David (but better), a prophet like Moses (but greater), and a priest like Melchizedek (but permanent). It isn't until the New Testament that we see the title *Son of God* (as discussed in chapter 2) applied to the Messiah. Such a title was largely off the prophetic radar. It would have been like announcing a smartphone in the Middle Ages. The exact phrase "Son of God" is nowhere to be found in the Old Testament. True, Israel had been called God's "son" in a collective sense (Hosea 11:1),[2] and his "firstborn son" (Exodus 4:22-23). It was kind of like saying "We're all God's children" at summer camp. Angels also received the title in their employee handbook (see Genesis 6:2, 4; Job 1:6; 2:1; 38:7). However, for an individual to claim this title was a different matter. That was either the height of blasphemy or . . . something entirely unprecedented in human history.[3]

Because the idea of the "Son of God" was so rare in the Old Testament, it's remarkable how common it is in the New Testament. The contrast could not be more striking. What was extraordinary and uncommon in the Hebrew Scriptures became central in the Christian writings. Three of the four Gospels identify Jesus as the Son of God in the very first chapter (see Mark 1:1; Luke 1:35; John 1:34), signaling to readers that this title is key to understanding Jesus' identity and mission. This immediate focus suggests that the early Christian community saw something unprecedented in Jesus' relationship to God the Father.

While Israel understood itself collectively as God's son through adoption and covenant, applying this title to an individual had profound and potentially blasphemous implications. To be a child of God—whether literally or figuratively—implied an intimate relationship, a special status, and even divine authority. When Jesus claimed this title, he was asserting himself as a divine agent, surpassing both the collective understanding of Israel and the political claims of Roman rulers (see appendix D).

The terms *Son of God* and *Christ/Messiah* are used interchangeably in the New Testament. Eleven times, the two terms appear in the same sentence, creating a link that would have surprised first-century Jewish readers, since *Son of God* was never part of the clear prophetic predictions of the Messiah. This connection marks an important theological development in early Christianity. The title *Christ* (or *Messiah*) traditionally implied expectations of political freedom and the restoration of Israel's fortunes. By associating it with *Son of God*, the New Testament writers broadened and redefined messianic ideas to include divine sonship in a way that went beyond traditional expectations.

So often we start with ourselves and define Jesus in relation to who we are or what we need. But we can't understand ourselves or our community without the context of the Messiah and his divine sonship. If we want to be God's children, it begins with knowing Jesus as the Son of God.

"WHO DO YOU SAY I AM?"

The angel Gabriel was the first to call Jesus "Son of God" (see Luke 1:35). Clearly, he had insider information. Next was the disciple Nathanael (see John 1:49) and John the Baptist (see John 1:34, KJV). Satan himself used the title when he challenged Jesus' identity during his testing in the wilderness (see Matthew 4:3, 6). This explains why the demon-possessed men from the Gadarenes used the title for Jesus in Matthew 8:29, which indicates this was a common practice among demons.

Angels and demons possessed information that wasn't immediately accessible to people. These supernatural beings recognized Jesus as the Son of God, not just through intellectual acknowledgment but with a fearful awareness of his authority over the spiritual realm. Their immediate submission (and, in the case of demons, outright terror) revealed an understanding of divine sonship that went beyond metaphor into practical reality.

The disciples recognized Jesus as the Son of God after he walked on water (see Matthew 14:33), a moment when Jesus showed undeniable authority over creation itself. This was no magic trick or illusion. Jesus did what only God could do by walking on the waves of the sea (see Job 9:8). So they acknowledged him as God's Son, with all the rights and privileges that come with it. He was revealing himself as God in what theologians call a theophany—a divine self-revelation. Soon after, in response to Jesus' question, Peter says, "You are the Messiah, the Son of the living God" (Matthew 16:16). This declaration marks a key moment in the Gospels, where the disciples shift from wondering about who Jesus is to marveling at who he is.

There comes a moment when Jesus asks us the same question he asked Peter: "What about you? Who do you say I am?" With the evidence before us on the pages of Scripture and written on our own hearts, how can we say anything other than "You are the Messiah, the Son of the living God"? Yet as was the case for Peter, the Messiah may be more than we ever imagined.

WHO DID JESUS SAY HE WAS?

Jesus approved of Peter's declaration. In fact, Jesus claimed the title "Son of God" for himself on several occasions (see John 5:25; 10:36; 11:4). This self-designation is significant considering his Jewish context, where such claims were seen as blasphemy (see John 10:33-38). Jesus' use of the title was neither casual nor accidental. It was purposeful and linked to claims of divine authority, such as giving life, executing judgment, and receiving the same honor as the Father.

Is it any wonder Caiaphas, the high priest, used this claim as one of the central points of his interrogation (see Matthew 26:63)? The Sanhedrin followed suit immediately afterward (see John 19:7). The religious authorities understood the implications of the claim. Jesus wasn't merely saying he was Israel's king; he was claiming to be their God. This self-identification was so central to the early church's message about Jesus that this was the point of John's entire Gospel, as expressed in the purpose statement for the book: "These are written that you may believe that Jesus is the Messiah, the Son of God, and that by believing you may have life in his name" (John 20:31).

Jesus' Jewish claim to be the "Son of God" was made in the long shadow cast by the Roman emperors. Augustus, the first Roman emperor, was called *dīvī fīlĭus* ("son of the divine") after Julius Caesar was posthumously deified. This designation continued with subsequent emperors, appearing on coins and inscriptions throughout the empire. For example, coins minted during Tiberius's reign (AD 14–37) bore the inscription *Ti Caesar Divi Avg F Avgvstvs*, shorthand for "Tiberius Caesar, son of the divine Augustus." This imperial propaganda created a charged political context for Christian claims about Jesus as Son of God.

There is a significant difference, however, between Jesus' claim and those of the emperors. First, the emperors were deified only after their deaths. Jesus was the first to claim a divine identity while alive. It wasn't until Caligula that any emperor claimed divinity *during their lifetime*, and he was notoriously delusional. Is it any wonder they called Jesus crazy (see Mark 3:20-22)?

You might call him crazy, but there's no sign of mental illness or maniacal self-centeredness. Jesus lived humbly and sacrificially, while these emperors used their power to indulge in immorality and excess. There was a vast difference between Jesus washing his disciples' feet and the emperors demanding worship. These human leaders had obvious ulterior motives—power, wealth, and control. Jesus' motive was salvation and shalom.

The emperors' failures betrayed their delusion. Their families were marked by trauma, their political legacy was filled with chaos, and the very empire crumbled under the weight of their moral depravity. Jesus, in contrast, proved his status as the Son of God by overcoming death through resurrection. No emperor ever did that. The resurrection served as vindication of Jesus' divine claims, transforming the apparent defeat of crucifixion into the ultimate victory—not merely for himself but for all who call him Lord. There is one passage that offers a helpful perspective on all this. Leave it to Luke, our detailed doctor-turned-historian, to connect some mind-blowing dots. In his genealogy (see Luke 3:38), he traces Jesus' family tree all the way back to Adam, who is called "son of God." As a Gentile, Luke shows that Jesus is not just a Jewish hero; he is the Savior of all humanity. What Adam marred in the garden, Jesus restored through an empty tomb. Where Adam's disobedience brought death, Jesus' obedience brought life. Not only is Jesus fully God, but he is also perfectly human—the perfect human, restoring what it means to be human. This God-man Jesus doesn't just save us *from* something (sin and death); he saves us *for* something (restored humanity in relationship with God).

WHAT THIS MEANS FOR US

Here's where it gets personal—really personal. Because Jesus is the Son of God (the authentic, verified version), we get to join the divine family network. This isn't just an honorary title or a spiritual participation trophy. This is about full adoption rights, with all privileges included!

Because Jesus became the new Adam, we can regain our status as sons and daughters of God. This goes beyond legal adoption; it signifies true transformation. Since Jesus is the Son of God (see Galatians 2:20; 4:4), we can become children of God (see Galatians 3:26; 4:5-7). Under Roman law, an adopted child received the same rights as a biological child—full stop. We're talking complete inheritance rights, a new identity, and a fresh start.

This new identity comes with both privileges and responsibilities:

- direct access to the Father, no heavenly receptionist needed (see Ephesians 2:18);
- joint inheritance with Christ—what a trust fund! (see Romans 8:17);
- family resemblance, in which we are transformed into his image (see Matthew 5:48; 2 Corinthians 3:18); and
- new family dynamics, in which every human-made barrier is broken down (see Ephesians 2:14-16; 5:8).

Being God's child isn't just about having your name on heaven's family registry; it's about living with divine DNA. When John says, "See what great love the Father has lavished on us, that we should be called children of God!" (1 John 3:1), he's inviting us to live in wide-eyed wonder at our new status. The church as the family of God provides a preview of the coming Kingdom, where God's children from every tribe, tongue, and nation will gather in perfect unity.

Here's the bottom line: *Son of God* isn't just another religious title to add to your theological database. It's the master key that unlocks everything else. Through Jesus, God didn't just send us a message—he sent us adoption papers. We have a new identity, a new family, a new way of being human.

Two thousand years after the Messiah's arrival onto the scene, this truth continues to change lives, one divine adoption at a time. It turns out that having the right ID isn't just important for getting through airport security—it's essential for eternal security. And thanks to Jesus, the Son of God, we all have access to the ultimate upgrade: becoming children of God ourselves.

7

THE MESSIAH NO ONE SAW COMING, PART 1

CEOs operate at a different level. They are often at the top of the building and the pay scale. Life is different up there, with unique views and expectations. When companies look for top leaders, their job descriptions differ from those of other roles. When a CEO position is posted, the responsibilities are usually implied by the title itself rather than explicitly listed. It's understood what a CEO does. The focus is instead on what additional qualities or unique skills are required for that particular organization to succeed.

What would a job posting for a messianic CEO look like? We've already covered the general roles in chapter 2: He was a *King* who established law and order and demanded loyalty and allegiance. More than just a King, he was a *Prophet* who spoke truth and confronted injustice. He was also a *Priest* who purified the people through his own sacrifice. This was evident from the prophetic predictions in the Old Testament, which were cited and explained in the New Testament.

This CEO of Israel, however, turned out to be much more than a mere leader of a nation. That's why Jesus went well beyond the roles of prophet, priest, and king. He exceeded every expectation in surprising and superlative ways. His unprecedented actions are unmistakable proof of his divine résumé. There are no less than seven stunning surprises about the Messiah Jesus.

SURPRISE #1: MESSIAH JESUS IS GREATER THAN HISTORICAL HEROES

Jesus wasn't just the Messiah to come; he was the culmination of all the biblical figures who came before him. He finished what they started and corrected what they corrupted. He is the New Adam, the predecessor of Abraham, the embodiment of Israel, the fulfillment of Moses, the promised King David, and the one greater than Solomon.

Imagine for a moment that we were talking not about the Messiah but about a US president. If the commander in chief claimed to be the new George Washington, greater than Abraham Lincoln, and more vital than FDR, he would be laughed out of DC. That shock would be minimal compared to a Jewish Messiah making the seismic claims that Jesus so boldly asserted.

What Jesus claimed is called *recapitulation*—the idea that history is summarized and fulfilled in him. Whenever something went awry in the Old Testament, it was made right through the Messiah in the New Testament. Adam sinned. Moses never entered the Promised Land. David wasn't allowed to build the Temple. Each time humans failed to fulfill what God asked them to do, Jesus repeated, completed, and perfected God's purpose and plans.

Adam

Adam failed to obey God in the garden, and the world has suffered ever since. Jesus became the new Adam—a perfected Adam—so he could restore us to a place where we can walk with God, as Adam did in the garden. Paul captures this idea in Romans 5:12-21, culminating in this declaration: "Just as sin reigned in death, so also grace might reign through righteousness to bring eternal life through Jesus Christ our Lord" (verse 21). Adam brought death into the world, and Jesus overcame death through the resurrection: "Since death came through a man, the resurrection of the dead comes also through a man. For as in Adam all die, so in Christ all will be made alive" (1 Corinthians 15:21-22). This isn't just a promise from the past; this is our future. Paul goes on to say that just as our earthly bodies resemble Adam's, so our heavenly bodies will resemble Jesus (see 1 Corinthians 15:49). What a promise! Jesus is more than we imagined.

Abraham

Abraham was the father of the Jewish people and ultimately of the Christian faith (see Romans 4). It's fair to say that no single person in world history has more people who look to him as their forefather. Anyone claiming to be comparable to Abraham in Jesus' day would have been threatened with execution. That's exactly what happened to Jesus during a particularly heated debate with Jewish leaders. He had the audacity to say, "Before

Abraham was born, I am!" (John 8:58). He was echoing Exodus 3:14, claiming the proper name for Yahweh. Is it any wonder they picked up stones to kill him?

The book of Hebrews dedicates an entire chapter to the idea that Jesus precedes Abraham (see Hebrews 7). This passage contends that Jesus is like Melchizedek, to whom Abraham paid tithes. Therefore, Jesus is not only greater than Abraham, but he is also the rightful fulfillment of the entire priesthood. Only by predating *and* replacing the Levitical priesthood could Jesus validly serve as both King and High Priest. No one imagined a Messiah like that.

Jacob (Israel)

Jacob was the father of the twelve tribes of Israel. His name is mentioned thirty-three times in Scripture as part of the triad of "Abraham, Isaac, and Jacob." He is such a significant figure that God changed his name to Israel. We typically think of Israel as a nation, but originally, Israel was a person whose descendants later became a nation.

Just as the nation of Israel came from Jacob, so, too, the nation was embodied in one man: Jesus. For example, Matthew 2:14-15 says, "[Joseph] got up, took the child and his mother during the night and left for Egypt, where he stayed until the death of Herod. And so was fulfilled what the Lord had said through the prophet: 'Out of Egypt I called my son.'" This prophecy from Hosea 11:1 shows how Jesus embodied the entire nation of Israel. The nation failed to be all God called them to be, but Jesus relived and restored their calling rightly.

The clearest comparison of Jesus to Jacob is when Jesus was sitting by a well that Jacob had dug (see John 4). The Samaritan woman asked him point-blank, "Are you greater than our father Jacob, who gave us the well and drank from it himself?" (verse 12). Jesus claimed he was. After all, the water he offered would become a spring of living water. Jesus didn't merely provide a well, as Jacob did; he makes us into life-giving springs: "Whoever drinks the water I give them will never thirst. Indeed, the water I give them will become in them a spring of water welling up to eternal life" (verse 14). That's far beyond any expectation.

Moses

God gave his laws through Moses, making him, far and away, the most important teacher of Israel. No rabbi dared contradict Moses. Nonetheless, in the Sermon on the Mount, six times in a single chapter, Jesus says, "You know what Moses said, but I say . . ." (see Matthew 5:21, 27, 31, 33, 38, 43). Essentially, he is expanding on the law of Moses. John makes the comparison clearly: "The law was given through Moses; grace and truth came through Jesus Christ" (John 1:17).

The comparison of Jesus to Moses goes beyond the law; it also includes manna. Moses gave the Israelites manna, but Jesus claimed to be the better bread from heaven (see John 6:31-35). Just as he offered living water to the woman at the well, he also said he is the bread of life: "Whoever eats my flesh and drinks my blood has eternal life, and I will raise them up at the last day" (John 6:54). This foreshadows Communion—his very body and blood are life-sustaining elements.

Such a superlative self-assessment might have seemed mentally unsound, but God confirmed Jesus' superiority over Moses at the transfiguration (see Matthew 17:1-13). This is corroborated in

Hebrews 3:3: "Jesus has been found worthy of greater honor than Moses, just as the builder of a house has greater honor than the house itself."

David

David was, without a doubt, the greatest king of Israel and the model for all subsequent kings. Before David died, God promised to raise the Messiah from his descendants (see 2 Samuel 7:12-16). As we've already seen, Jesus called out this promise to the Pharisees (see Matthew 22:41-46). He made the clear connection that he was greater than David because he was not just David's descendant but also God's Son.

The New Testament starts with Jesus' genealogy in Matthew, emphasizing David. Crowds called out to Jesus as the "Son of David" (Matthew 9:27; 15:22; 20:30-31; 21:9). Both Peter and Paul identify Jesus as the Son of David in their first recorded sermons (see Acts 2:30-36; 13:22-23). In the last chapter of the Bible, Jesus made this declaration about himself: "I, Jesus . . . am the Root and the Offspring of David, and the bright Morning Star" (Revelation 22:16). Jesus the Messiah is not just the king of Israel; he is the King of kings, enthroned in heaven.

Solomon (and Jonah)

One of the clearest examples of the comparison of Solomon (and Jonah) to Jesus comes from Matthew 12. The scribes and Pharisees asked Jesus for a sign to prove his messianic claims. The only sign he offered was his coming resurrection: "As Jonah was three days and three nights in the belly of a huge fish, so the Son of Man will be three days and three nights in the heart of the earth" (verse 40). Jesus concluded with these words: "Something greater than Jonah is here" (verse 41).

He then turned to Solomon: "The Queen of the South will rise at the judgment with this generation and condemn it; for she came from the ends of the earth to listen to Solomon's wisdom, and now *something greater than Solomon is here*" (Matthew 12:42, emphasis added). Solomon was the wisest man who ever lived; Jesus was wisdom itself (see 1 Corinthians 1:24).

The other comparison to Solomon also involves a request for a sign and a promise of resurrection. In John 2:13-22, we read about Jesus cleansing the Temple. The religious leaders were furious: "What sign can you show us to prove your authority to do all this?" (verse 18). Jesus replied, "Destroy this temple, and I will raise it again in three days" (verse 19). Solomon was commanded by God to build the Temple. That Temple, it turned out, was temporary, and it was destroyed long before Jesus was born. It was later replaced by another Temple, which was also destined for destruction. Compare that to Jesus' temple—his body. He was raised to eternal glory. Just as Jacob (Israel) became a nation, so, too, Jesus' resurrected body became the foundation of the new temple, built not out of stone but out of God's people (see Ephesians 2:19-22; 1 Corinthians 3:9-17; 1 Peter 2:4-6). Just as the Temple was the place where the Jewish people met God, Jesus is the place we meet God. This far exceeds any hopes or dreams anyone had of the Messiah.

Elijah

The acts and miracles of Jesus are uncannily similar to Elijah's. Both raised a widow's son from the dead (see 1 Kings 17:17-24;

Luke 7:11-17), multiplied food (see 1 Kings 17:8-16; Mark 6:30-44), exerted control over the rain (see 1 Kings 17:1; 18:41-45; Mark 4:35-41), confronted rulers (see 1 Kings 18; Luke 23), and ascended to heaven (see 2 Kings 2:11; Acts 1:9-11).

Is it any wonder that people compared Jesus to Elijah (see Matthew 16:13-14)? But God did not see them as peers. When Moses and Elijah stood with Jesus on the Mount of Transfiguration, Peter wanted to honor them all equally. God interrupted, saying, "This is my Son, whom I love; with him I am well pleased. Listen to him!" (Matthew 17:5). Jesus isn't merely *like* Elijah—they can't even be put on the same plane, according to God himself. Peter, James, and John had to learn that lesson on the Mount of Transfiguration. Perhaps we need to pay attention to this lesson too.

Greater than Our Own Heroes

Jesus corrected what the Old Testament heroes left incomplete and perfected the virtue for which they were known. Who could have guessed that even with the prophecies at hand, he would exceed any single hero of the faith, let alone the sum of all of them? The patriarchs and kings may seem very distant. We are, however, closer to them than we often imagine. Like ancient Israel, we want an earthly hero to fight our battles for us. We want a political figure or social icon to represent us. Since Jesus isn't visible to us and his actions aren't always obvious, it can be tempting to follow someone with more charisma or a flashier presentation or greater social media influence. In our image-driven society, there's a pull to hitch our identity to someone who follows Jesus rather than Jesus himself. But anyone other than the Messiah is, at best, a mere shadow of the real thing—and they will inevitably disappoint us.

SURPRISE #2: MESSIAH JESUS EMBODIES THE SYMBOLS OF JUDAISM

It is extraordinary that Jesus fulfilled the central stories of Israel's most influential figures. Yet even that wasn't the full extent of his messianic achievements. Jesus also embodied the sacred structures and institutions that defined Judaism: Temple worship, Sabbath, Passover, and Torah.

Pause for a moment and let that sink in. He is not merely the embodiment of Israel's heroes; he is the fulfillment of all their elements of worship. This would be like a modern American political figure declaring, "I am the land of the free and the home of the brave; I am Uncle Sam, the flag, 'The Star-Spangled Banner,' the Fourth of July, baseball, and apple pie." This would be a hilarious skit on SNL if Jesus hadn't declared it with divine authority and backed it up with his own death and resurrection.

Temple

As already noted, Jesus is the embodied Temple (see John 2:19-22). This sacred structure was regarded as the center of God's presence on earth. As the site for annual pilgrimage, it served as the symbolic hub of God's people. In Jesus' day, anyone who threatened the Temple would be beaten, possibly executed, and labeled an enemy of the state.[1]

It was here, on this sacred ground, that God met the high priest once a year to receive the blood of atonement, sprinkled on the Ark of the Covenant. That blood-splattered lid was called "the mercy seat" (Exodus 25:17-22, KJV). The same word (translated into Greek) is used in Romans 3:25 to describe Jesus: "God presented Christ as a sacrifice of atonement [referring to the literal place of atonement], through the shedding of his blood."

Jesus' own body is the living temple. After he rose from the dead, his followers, the church, became the body of Christ. Whenever Paul described the church as the temple (see 1 Corinthians 3:16-17; 6:19; 2 Corinthians 6:16; Ephesians 2:21), he used the word for *temple* proper, referring particularly to the Holy of Holies, not the entire temple complex.[2] The people of the Messiah are now the place where God dwells on earth.

Sabbath

Few traditions are more quintessentially Jewish than the Sabbath. This day of rest defines Jewish identity. It was established not in the Mosaic law but in the garden (see Genesis 2:2-3). It was later included in the Ten Commandments and became a lasting tenet in Jewish faith and tradition.

It's a big deal, and it led to big fights during Jesus' ministry. The Gospels record seven separate times when the religious leaders accosted Jesus for "violating" the Sabbath. While the Pharisees saw the Sabbath as a set of rules to be followed, Jesus used it for healing and refreshment. On one occasion, he was questioned for allowing his disciples to pick heads of grain as they walked through a field on the Sabbath (see Mark 2:23-28). It was a quick snack during their walk, but the Pharisees observing them were outraged. Their overly strict (and unbiblical) rules declared this a violation of the restriction against harvesting (plucking heads of grain), winnowing (rolling them in their hands to loosen the kernels), and winnowing again (blowing off the chaff).

The Pharisees' legalism clearly goes beyond the biblical purpose of the Sabbath, as Jesus pointed out. This encounter reached its peak with one of Jesus' most remarkable (and controversial) statements: "The Son of Man is Lord even of the Sabbath" (Mark 2:28). He wasn't just claiming to be greater than Moses; he was asserting equality with the Creator. He is the Judge of the Sabbath, an institution that dates back to Eden. That's quite a claim.

Passover

The annual Passover festival commemorates Israel's Independence Day, when they were freed from captivity in Egypt. There were very specific rules about how the meal for this celebration should be prepared. The centerpiece of the meal was the Passover lamb. It was the main course, not just in a culinary way but theologically too. On their last night in Egypt, Moses instructed each Israelite family to sacrifice a one-year-old male lamb, without blemish, at twilight. It was to be roasted whole, without breaking any bones, and completely consumed. Most importantly, its blood was to be painted on the doorposts of their homes, marking them as off-limits to the angel of death.

Thus, the Israelites avoided the tenth plague, the death of the firstborn son. This broke their enemies' resistance and secured their freedom (see Exodus 12). The parallels to Jesus are clear—so clear, in fact, that at a Passover meal the night before he died, Jesus established the Lord's Supper with these words: "This is my blood of the covenant, which is poured out for many" (Mark 14:24).

With this, he replaced the entire Old Testament sacrificial system with his own death. This should not have been a surprise, since John the Baptist had predicted this three years earlier, declaring about Jesus: "Look, the Lamb of God, who takes away the sin of the world!" (John 1:29).

Torah

From a Jewish perspective, the law of God was a divine privilege for the people. Paul states this in Romans 3:1-2: "What advantage, then, is there in being a Jew, or what value is there in circumcision? Much in every way! First of all, the Jews have been entrusted with the very words of God." The rules God gave his people showed his special love for them. That's why the Torah was held in such high regard. Even today, it is treated with reverence in the synagogue and regarded as an object of divine beauty.

For anyone to compare their words or their life to the Word of God would have provoked a fierce reaction. Nonetheless, Jesus' teachings clarified the law (see Mark 2:27-28), expanded the law (see Matthew 5:21-28), and in some cases even modified the law (see Mark 7:19). Moreover, his sinless life perfectly embodied the law, and his death fulfilled its requirements (see Matthew 5:17). This is why his words serve as the foundation for a successful life (see Matthew 7:24-27).

It's no surprise, therefore, that John 1:1, which clearly echoes Genesis 1:1, identifies Jesus as the *Logos* (Word) of God: "In the beginning was the Word, and the Word was with God, and the Word was God" (John 1:1). Even before his incarnation, Jesus was the Word of God. Since God created the world through his Word, Jesus is the source of creation (see Colossians 1:16). And unlike the law, Jesus is more than a book; he is God become flesh: "The Word became flesh and made his dwelling among us. We have seen his glory, the glory of the one and only Son, who came from the Father, full of grace and truth" (John 1:14).

The Unimaginable Jesus

Jesus embodied every essential element of the Jewish faith. He wasn't merely the quintessential Israelite; he's the embodiment of Judaism—its heroes and its symbols. Yet he is more. The Messiah wasn't just a national figure; he's a global one. He's the sacred place where we meet with God, he's the rest our souls long for, he's the sacrifice that liberates us from the curse of death, he's the fulfillment of every prophecy, and he is all that for all people, for all time.

Could such a Messiah really exist? As followers of Jesus, we're staking our lives on the fact that he does. We take literally the words of the apostle Paul: He is "able to do immeasurably more than all we ask or imagine, according to his power that is at work within us" (Ephesians 3:20). Jesus is more than we ever imagined. He alone can carry us through any challenges that lie ahead.

Recognizing that Jesus goes beyond our expectations, we'd be wise to do a regular inventory of our habits and rituals to ensure that they're focused upward, not inward. Put another way, we need to make sure that we elevate Jesus to CEO of our lives and that we're reporting to him, not the other way around.

8

THE MESSIAH NO ONE SAW COMING, PART 2

The elderly man flying coach from New York to Dublin wouldn't catch your eye for a second. You'd probably mistake him for a mid-level manager because of his simple clothes and inexpensive watch. You might assume he's a grandfather visiting family abroad. Most likely, you wouldn't even notice him behind his newspaper. The flight attendants definitely didn't make any fuss over him.

The rest of his life wasn't glamorous either. He lived in a rented apartment, carried his belongings in a plastic bag, and used public transportation. When he ate out, it was at diners, not five-star restaurants. His friends knew him as frugal—almost to a fault.

What a casual observer might not have realized is that this penny-pinching old guy was Chuck Feeney, a wildly successful mogul who cofounded Duty Free Shoppers, the airport retail empire. Throughout his life, he made over $8 billion, which he carefully and secretly donated through his anonymous foundation, the Atlantic Philanthropies. Over the course of almost forty years, he funded universities across Ireland, supported peace initiatives in Northern Ireland, built hospitals in Vietnam, and improved countless lives across five continents.

When he finally revealed his identity as a philanthropist in 1997, he had long since pledged all his past and future profits to the foundation, which had already donated $600 million. The man everyone overlooked on economy flights had been looking after the overlooked of this world. Similarly—but on a much larger scale—Jesus the Messiah is far more than what meets the eye. In this chapter, we'll attempt to see him more fully by exploring five more jaw-dropping surprises that reveal Jesus as greater than anyone imagined.

SURPRISE #3: MESSIAH JESUS SUFFERS FOR THE NATION

Before Jesus arrived, the idea of a Suffering Servant was on no one's messianic radar. The Messiah might cause his enemies to suffer, sure. But he himself? He would be too powerful to be harmed.

If you look for evidence of a Suffering Servant in the Old Testament, you'll find only two passages that predicted a Messiah touched by pain. Both predictions were so unexpected that the early rabbis actually rewrote them. Here is what that looked like.

Zechariah 12:10 says, "I will pour out on the house of David and the inhabitants of Jerusalem a spirit of grace and supplication. They will look on me, the one they have pierced, and they will mourn for him as one mourns for an only child." Clearly, this is God speaking—who else could pour out a "spirit of grace"? But how could God be pierced? Who is tall enough to reach him? Who is strong enough to hurt him? The idea that God would suffer was unthinkable. So the translators of the Septuagint replaced the word *pierced* with a similar-sounding Hebrew word meaning "danced."[1] They depicted God's enemies as dancing in derision. The idea of God suffering was so strange that they changed the biblical text to make it more understandable.

They did something similar with Isaiah 53. This prophetic song clearly celebrates a Suffering Servant. The rabbis altered the meaning of Isaiah 53 in their paraphrased version (called a Targum). Here's one example. Isaiah 53:3 says, "He was despised and rejected by mankind, a man of suffering, and familiar with pain. Like one from whom people hide their faces he was despised, and we held him in low esteem." Their paraphrase reversed this: "Then the glory of all the kingdoms will be for contempt and cease; they will be faint and mournful . . . they are despised and not esteemed."[2] Instead of the Messiah suffering, he causes suffering for his enemies.

A suffering Messiah was a complete contradiction in Judaism. Nobody predicted it . . . except Jesus. Just a few days before Jesus was to die, the Jewish leaders challenged him to justify his actions, especially the clearing of the Temple. He responded with a parable about a vineyard (see Matthew 21:23-46).

Here's the basic storyline: A vineyard owner rented out his vineyard. At harvest, he sent his servants to collect his share of the profits, but the tenants kept killing them. Finally, the owner sent his own son, thinking, *Surely, they'll respect him.* But they didn't. They beat and killed him as well. Jesus' parable was clearly autobiographical. When he asked his opponents what they thought should happen to those tenants, they angrily answered, "Those villains deserve to die." Then it suddenly dawned on them, *He's talking about us!* They were apoplectic.

To add insult to injury, Jesus quoted a prophecy from Psalm 118:22-23: "The stone the builders rejected has become the cornerstone; the Lord has done this, and it is marvelous in our eyes" (Matthew 21:42). Clearly, a violent rejection of God's Son was inevitable. What makes this fascinating is that the Hebrew word for "stone" (*eben*) and the word for "son" (*ben*) sound almost identical. The slightest breath is all that separates them. They were so similar that the rabbis understood the word *eben* ("stone") to be a metaphor for *ben* ("son").[3] Jesus' interpretation of Psalm 118:22-23 said nothing their own rabbis hadn't already taught.

A suffering Messiah was hard to find in the ancient texts. But it was there for anyone with eyes to see. The God above and beyond human pain entered our world and embraced the harsh realities of the human condition. He knows what it's like to be hurt, to suffer, to face an unjustified death. While we avoid pain, he embraced it for our sake.

SURPRISE #4: MESSIAH JESUS WELCOMES ENEMIES

The usual descriptions of the Messiah in the Old Testament resembled King David's psalms, asking God to defeat his enemies (see Isaiah 7; Daniel 7:1-14; Jeremiah 23:1-7). They had hopes for divine revenge and visions of enemies getting what they deserved—violent language that seems fitting for an R-rated action movie.

Those expectations of divine retribution were completely shattered by Jesus the Messiah. Instead of attacking his opponents, he taught such "offensive" things as "Love your enemies and pray for those who persecute you" (Matthew 5:44). How could Jesus' fellow Jews have been so far off from his messianic vision? Were they reading the same predictions?

They were, but Jesus' contemporaries interpreted them through their own cultural expectations and desires (a practice we are guilty of as well). Here's an important example. God's promise to Abraham laid the foundation for the Hebrew people. Four times, Genesis records God's promise to bless the whole world through Abraham (see Genesis 12:1-3; 22:18; 26:4; 28:14). The common interpretation was that outsiders who converted to Judaism—adopting Jewish laws, following Hebrew customs, and living in Israel—would be blessed. However, there were a few glimpses of an outward focus of Abraham's promise, suggesting that the blessing was not about outsiders joining in but about insiders going out. For example, Isaiah 49:6 says, "It is too small a thing for you to be my servant to restore the tribes of Jacob and bring back those of Israel I have kept. I will also make you a light for the Gentiles, that my salvation may reach to the ends of the earth."

This tension is clearly shown in the book of Jonah. Jonah highlights the prevailing attitude of Israelites toward outsiders at the time—they were more likely to pray for the destruction of an idolatrous city such as Nineveh than for its salvation. Yet Jesus' messianic calling aligned with God's vision for outsiders, even those considered Israel's enemies. Jesus' critique of Capernaum, where he did many of his miracles, demonstrates his perspective: "You, Capernaum, will you be lifted to the heavens? No, you will go down to Hades. For if the miracles that were performed in you had been performed in Sodom, it would have remained to this day. But I tell you that it will be more bearable for Sodom on the day of judgment than for you" (Matthew 11:23-24). In other words, God is more concerned with the state of people's hearts than with their passports.

This is one of the most important aspects of Jesus the Messiah. The primary Jewish hope was that the Messiah would restore the twelve tribes. Jesus did so, but in an unexpected way. Instead of bringing back the scattered tribes of ethnic Jews, he expanded Israel's borders to include all languages, tribes, and nations. Being part of God's family is no longer based primarily on ethnicity. Inclusion is based on allegiance to God, just like it was for Abraham. Those who share Abraham's faith are adopted into his family tree.

In the church today, we have our own kinds of spiritual snobbery—unspoken tests to determine who's in and who's out. But that's not the way of Jesus. Whether you're a first-generation Christian or there have been pastors in your family tree for generations, whether you're from a culture where Christianity is common or from a people group where following Jesus puts you in the minority, you are welcome at the table. The Messiah's invitation is open to all who pledge their allegiance to him.

SURPRISE #5: MESSIAH JESUS COMBINES KINGSHIP AND PRIESTHOOD

As we discussed in chapter 2, Jewish priests could only come from the tribe of Levi, and kings could only come from the tribe of Judah. So how could the Messiah be both a priest and a king?

The clue to this puzzle, according to the book of Hebrews, can be found in the mysterious figure named Melchizedek. He lived at the same time as Abraham, and he was both king of Salem (later Jerusalem) and a priest. Hebrews 7 explains that Abraham paid a tithe to Melchizedek: "This Melchizedek was king of Salem and priest of God Most High. He met Abraham returning from the defeat of the kings and blessed him" (verse 1). Verse 10 says, "When Melchizedek met Abraham, Levi was still in the body of his ancestor." How can Jesus be both King and Priest? Because, like Melchizedek, he came before both Levi and David. Jesus said it himself: "Before Abraham was born, I am!" (John 8:58). Jesus, the fulfillment of Melchizedek, precedes and supersedes both Levi and David. Jesus the Messiah is before and above all priests and kings. That's why he can be both.

Twice, Jesus referenced his dual role as king and priest. When the Pharisees accused Jesus of letting his disciples pick grain and eat it on the Sabbath, he pointed out that King David, while fleeing from Saul, ate the priestly showbread, which was only allowed for priests (see 1 Samuel 21:6). Jesus' reasoning was straightforward: If David could do that, how much more should Jesus and his followers be allowed to do so? After all, Jesus was greater than both David and the priesthood. He then made this jaw-dropping claim: "I tell you that something greater than the temple is here" (Matthew 12:6). The Temple, built by king Solomon, was where priests served in God's presence. Jesus claimed to be greater than all of that.

Fast-forward to the last week of Jesus' life. It was finally time for Jesus to publicly declare his messianic identity (see Luke 20:41-44). His confirmation came from Psalm 110:1: "The

LORD says to my Lord: 'Sit at my right hand until I make your enemies a footstool for your feet.'" As we've already seen, this passage portrays the Messiah as David's Lord. But the context reveals even more, which the religious leaders knew perfectly well. Psalm 110:4 continues, "The LORD has sworn and will not change his mind: 'You are a priest forever, in the order of Melchizedek.'"

Prior to Jesus, the Jewish people focused on the Messiah as King, which made them more likely to miss their Savior as the Suffering Servant. Today, we tend to make the opposite mistake. We see Jesus clearly as the Savior of our souls for eternity, but is he truly the Lord of our lives right now? It's easy to answer automatically, "Oh, sure, he's my Lord—I go to church, read my Bible, and pray." But I would argue that he's more likely to ask about your relationships, your financial commitments, and your service to the least and the lost than the religious duties you perform in the presence of other Christians. When you fight with your spouse or your roommate, do you respond to the situation or the lordship of the Messiah? Are you raising your kids based on loyalty to the Messiah or to a sports team? Does your spending reflect a messianic allegiance to sacrificial giving or culturally conditioned consumerism? There are very real, practical considerations for anyone who declares Jesus as their King.

SURPRISE #6: MESSIAH JESUS WILL BRING WORLD HISTORY TO ITS END

When ancient Jews thought about the Messiah, they weren't just dreaming of a better government or more prosperous times. They were expecting a national hero who would finally settle the score, defeat their enemies, and bring justice to the nation. This would be the ultimate courtroom drama, where every nation and individual would stand trial for their treatment of God's people.

Jesus boldly claimed this role, but with an unexpected twist. Instead of immediately unleashing divine judgment on Israel's enemies, he introduced what scholars call the "already/not yet" Kingdom. The Judge had arrived, but the final verdict was delayed to give his enemies a chance to become allies.

We're currently living in this tension, waiting for the dramatic finish line when the Messiah comes a second time. Matthew 24–25 provides a vivid description of "the last days," when the world spirals into chaos: wars erupting, famines devastating nations, false messiahs deceiving many, and Jesus' followers facing fierce persecution. Yet these birth pangs will ultimately lead to his triumphant return.

Leaders in the early church, including John in the book of Revelation, elaborated on this theme with vivid imagery about Jesus returning as the Warrior-King on a white horse, bringing history to its dramatic climax. This idea wasn't entirely new—it built on the rich foundation of prophets like Daniel, who saw "one like a son of man, coming with the clouds of heaven" (Daniel 7:13); Ezekiel, who witnessed dry bones coming to life (see Ezekiel 37:1-14); and Zechariah, who foresaw a day when "the Lord will be king over the whole earth" (Zechariah 14:9).

This end-times dimension had always existed at the edges of messianic expectation, but Jesus placed it at the center. He came not just to bring immediate political deliverance but to serve as the cosmic cornerstone of human history. The judgment he promised wasn't just punitive but transformative—it wasn't just an ending but a complete recalibration. As Isaiah prophesied, "he will judge between the nations and will settle disputes for many peoples" (Isaiah 2:4), establishing ultimate justice and resolving history's accumulated wrongs.

How often, when we pray, do we expect something smaller than what God has to offer? We think Jesus will work in predictable, controllable ways. But in reality, he's usually up to something much more disruptive—and more redemptive—than we can fathom. As C. S. Lewis puts it,

> Imagine yourself as a living house. God comes in to rebuild that house. At first, perhaps, you can understand what He is doing. He is getting the drains right and stopping the leaks in the roof and so on: you knew that those jobs needed doing and so you are not surprised. But presently he starts knocking the house about in a way that hurts abominably and does not seem to make sense. What on earth is He up to? The explanation is that He is building quite a different house from the one you thought of—throwing out a new wing here, putting on an extra floor there, running up towers, making courtyards. You thought you were going to be made into a decent little cottage: but He is building a palace. He intends to come and live in it Himself.[4]

When the Messiah knocks at our door, there is likely a wrecking ball behind him. He will do far more than we imagine, and it will cost far more than we had budgeted. He gives everything, changes everything, and demands everything.

SURPRISE #7: MESSIAH JESUS IS YAHWEH

Perhaps the greatest messianic surprise of all was Jesus' deity. The Messiah wasn't just a great man—he was the God-man. This surpassed the imaginative limits of any Jewish expectations of the Messiah. He was supposed to be many things—King, Priest, Prophet, Liberator, Judge, Warrior. But Yahweh in the flesh was beyond human imagination.

Yet the evidence is there, clear as day, scattered throughout the New Testament. Thomas (the "Doubter") is the first one recorded to call him "my Lord and my God" (John 20:28). Peter, in his first public sermon, proclaimed him "Lord and Messiah" (Acts 2:36) and affirmed the same in his letter: "Simon Peter, a servant and apostle of Jesus Christ, to those who through the righteousness of our God and Savior Jesus Christ have received a faith as precious as ours" (2 Peter 1:1). John wasted no time asserting Jesus' deity in John 1:18: "No one has ever seen God, but the one and only Son, who is himself God and is in closest relationship with the Father, has made him known." Multiple times, the apostle Paul equated Jesus the Messiah with Yahweh (see Romans 9:5; 2 Thessalonians 1:12; Titus 2:13). The writer of Hebrews is no exception, quoting Psalm 45:6 to describe Jesus: "Your throne, O God, will last for ever and ever; a scepter of justice will be the scepter of your kingdom" (Hebrews 1:8).

These consistent declarations of deity didn't originate from human imagination. Although the resurrection is the final and definitive proof of Jesus' divine nature (see Psalm 16:10; Luke 24:46), there are clues throughout Jesus' ministry that clearly point to his deity:

- Jesus claimed to be the fulfillment of every major Old Testament hero and institution of Israel (see chapter 7). This includes Adam, Abraham, Jacob, Moses, David, Solomon, Elijah, and Jonah. He is the embodiment of the Temple, the Torah, Israel, the Passover, and the Sabbath.
- Jesus claimed the authority to make the final judgment (see Matthew 7:22-23; 16:27; 25:31-46; John 5:24-30) and to forgive sins (see Luke 5:17-26; 7:47-50).
- Jesus called himself the Son of Man (see Daniel 7:13-14). This explains why he allowed people to bow in worship to him (Mark 1:40; 10:17; Matthew 9:18; 15:25; 17:14; 26:6-13; Luke 5:8-9; 7:36-50; 19:35-40), even though it was strictly forbidden for Jews to bow to humans, or even to angels (see Acts 10:25-26; Revelation 19:10; 22:8-9).
- Three times, Jesus alluded to his deity. First, he acknowledged his preexistence with the very name of God: "Before Abraham was born, I am!" (John 8:58). Second, he identified himself as David's Lord (see Matthew 22:41-46, citing Psalm 110:1). Third, he declared, "All things have been committed to me by my Father. No one knows the Son except the Father, and no one knows the Father except the Son and those to whom the Son chooses to reveal him" (Matthew 11:27). The divine implications are impossible to overlook.

Given these claims and actions, it's clear why Jesus' followers proclaimed him divine. Isaiah 9:6 says, "To us a child is born, to us a son is given, and the government will be on his shoulders. And he will be called Wonderful Counselor, Mighty God,

Everlasting Father, Prince of Peace." The earthly descriptions of the Messiah (child, ruler, counselor, Prince of Peace) are listed along with his divine attributes (Mighty God, Everlasting Father). While rabbis typically interpreted this prophecy as being fulfilled by two separate entities, there's no grammatical or linguistic reason to treat them as two different people.[5]

Jesus and the apostles clarified what the Old Testament writers hint at: The Messiah is more than a man; he is also divine.

EXCEEDING OUR EXPECTATIONS

The evidence is clear: Jesus surpassed all messianic expectations of his time. He replaced the idea of a conquering hero with that of a Suffering Servant. Instead of defeating his enemies, he gave them the chance to become his allies. He shifted Abraham's blessing from being an exclusive gift to insiders to being an outward invitation to anyone who embraces the gift of God. Instead of merely gathering the twelve tribes, he expanded Israel's borders.

Jesus' preexistence enabled him to merge both kingship and priesthood, as Melchizedek once did, into his messianic role. But the greatest surprise surpassed all others: his deity. Jesus the Messiah is the I Am. The humble carpenter from Nazareth proved to be more than anyone dared imagine.

Just as Jesus exceeded the expectations of his day, he goes beyond the expectations of our day as well. He didn't come to make your life marginally better. He came to extend the margins of your life infinitely. We have more brothers and sisters than we dreamed. Our houses and lands extend to a new heaven and a new earth. Our King's forgiveness is infinite; his grace knows no bounds. What we imagined to be true about ourselves is rewritten because our identity is found in his eternal essence. We are not divine, but we share in his divine nature, imprinted by the very Spirit of God. We are sons and daughters of the divine Messiah.

9

THE COMEBACK THAT PROVED HIS MESSIAHSHIP

A few years ago, I was sitting in a coffee shop working on an Easter sermon when I overheard a conversation at the next table. A college-aged woman was explaining to her friend that even though she was a Christian, she didn't "fully buy into it."

"I mean, I can appreciate Jesus as a great teacher," she said, stirring her latte. "His ideas about loving others are beautiful. But the whole resurrection thing? That's where they lose me. Do people actually believe that? I think it's supposed to be a metaphor about how his teachings would live on after he died."

I resisted the urge to interject, but her comment stayed with me. For this young woman, and for countless others in our culture, the resurrection is an optional add-on to Christianity, a belief that modern people can politely set aside while still claiming Jesus.

What I wanted to say to her—what I restrained myself from blurting across the coffee shop—was this: "The resurrection isn't an elective for the Christian faith; it's the foundation for everything we believe about Jesus. Without it, there is no Christianity."

That's true in some ways you might expect, but it's also true in a less obvious way: Without the resurrection, there is no Messiah.

One of the most significant ways Western culture has reduced Jesus from the revolutionary Messiah to a personalized savior is in our understanding of the resurrection. We've often narrowed its significance to either a metaphor for spiritual renewal or a promise of our own future resurrection. Both perspectives, while containing important truth, miss a central meaning: The resurrection marked Jesus' coronation as King. He didn't just rise from the dead; he ascended to the throne.

THE RESURRECTION AS THE LINCHPIN

There is a fun Latin phrase for linchpin: *sine qua non.* It means "without which, not"—it describes something necessary or essential; without it, the whole thing would fall apart. Here are some examples of *sine qua non*:

- Sarcasm is the *sine qua non* of surviving holiday dinners with extended family.
- Caffeine is the *sine qua non* of parenting toddlers.
- A preplanned exit strategy is the *sine qua non* of office parties.

You get the idea.

Paul understood that the resurrection is the *sine qua non* of the Christian faith. "If Christ has not been raised, our preaching is useless and so is your faith. More than that, we are then found to be false witnesses about God, for we have testified about God that he raised Christ from the dead. . . . And if Christ has not been raised, your faith is futile; you are still in your sins" (1 Corinthians 15:14-15, 17). Paul didn't sugarcoat this truth about the resurrection: If Jesus wasn't raised from the dead, our faith is futile and we are to be pitied. The resurrection isn't an optional add-on to Christianity; it's the foundation everything else stands on.

So why is the resurrection so essential?

THE PERSONAL SIGNIFICANCE OF THE RESURRECTION

For believers, the promise and the power of the resurrection is deeply personal. Without the resurrection, as Paul notes, we would still be in our sins. The resurrection serves as something of a divine validation of our forgiveness. Without it, death would remain undefeated, and our hope for eternal life would be groundless. Without Jesus' resurrection, we would have no assurance that his promises to us will be fulfilled.

The resurrection promises that death is not the end of our story; it guarantees our own future resurrection. It assures us that our loved ones who have died in Christ are with him now. For believers who have stood at the graveside of a loved one, the reality that Jesus is alive is an anchor of hope. I'll never forget holding the hand of a church member as her husband of sixty-two years took his final breath. Through her tears, she whispered, "He's with Jesus now. And one day I'll see him again." What she expressed was not wishful thinking but a certain promise, guaranteed by the reality of Jesus walking out of his grave.

The New Testament consistently connects Jesus' resurrection to our own future resurrection. Paul assured the Corinthians,

"Christ has indeed been raised from the dead, the firstfruits of those who have fallen asleep" (1 Corinthians 15:20). The term *firstfruits* refers to the initial portion of a harvest, which serves as something of a down payment on the full harvest to come. Jesus' resurrection was not an isolated miracle but the beginning of a resurrection harvest that will include all who belong to him.

For believers facing their own mortality, this promise provides profound comfort. While I was working on this chapter, I called a longtime friend who is fighting stage 4 cancer and is nearing his final days. I asked him about how his cancer journey has impacted his understanding of the resurrection. He told me, "The only reason I'm not afraid is because I know Jesus rose from the dead. He conquered death and is waiting for me on the other side." I could hear the depth of his conviction in his voice.

Beyond the hope of future resurrection, the New Testament also teaches that the power that raised Jesus is available to us today. Paul prayed that believers would know "his incomparably great power for us who believe. That power is the same as the mighty strength he exerted when he raised Christ from the dead" (Ephesians 1:19-20). This isn't abstract theology; it's the promise that the same divine power that conquered death is at work in our lives amid our daily struggles.

The personal dimension of the resurrection is not untrue or trivial; this hope is a precious gift that has sustained believers through grief and hardship for centuries. The challenge is that we focus so much on its personal meaning that we miss something equally important: The resurrection is the linchpin validating Jesus' messiahship.

A KING WHO WOULD NEVER DIE

One of the Jewish expectations for the Messiah was that he would not die but would live forever. This expectation was rooted in Scripture:

- Psalm 16:10 promises, "You will not abandon me to the realm of the dead, nor will you let your faithful one see decay."
- Psalm 102:27 declares of God's anointed, "You remain the same, and your years will never end."
- Isaiah 9:7 proclaims about the coming King, "Of the greatness of his government and peace there will be no end."

These Scriptures, and others,[1] led the Jews to believe that the Messiah would live forever. So when Jesus began speaking about his coming death, his disciples were horrified because this seemed to contradict the expectation that the Messiah would not die. Peter rebuked him. "'Never, Lord!' he said. 'This shall never happen to you!'" (Matthew 16:22). Peter wasn't just expressing concern for Jesus' welfare; he was revealing his theological confusion. How could Jesus be the Messiah if he was going to die?

Even after three years with Jesus and hearing his predictions about his death and resurrection, the disciples couldn't reconcile the idea of a dying Messiah with their expectations. When Jesus was crucified, their messianic hopes were shattered. As the two disciples on the road to Emmaus lamented, "We had hoped that he was the one who was going to redeem Israel" (Luke 24:21).

The past tense speaks volumes. Jesus' death had seemingly disqualified him as the Messiah in their eyes.

Anyone who claimed to be the Messiah but eventually died would be proven false. But how could someone live long enough to prove they wouldn't die? Even if it were possible for an ordinary human to live for two hundred years, or even a thousand, that would not be a guarantee that they would live forever.

If Jesus had died and stayed dead, he would just be another failed messianic pretender, one of many who rose and fell in first-century Palestine. His teachings might still be valuable, his example still inspiring, but his claim to be the Messiah would be invalidated.

RESOLVED BY THE RESURRECTION

The death and resurrection of Jesus resolved this paradox once and for all.

First, he died—and not quietly or ambiguously. He died in the most public, undeniable, and humiliating way possible. His execution was witnessed by crowds, confirmed by professional executioners, and certified by Roman officials. As he hung on the cross, his opponents mocked him: "'He saved others,' they said, 'but he can't save himself! He's the king of Israel! Let him come down now from the cross, and we will believe in him'" (Matthew 27:42). They didn't realize it, but they were acknowledging the very paradox Jesus was about to resolve.

Second, Jesus satisfied the Jewish understanding of death. In Jewish tradition, only after three days was a person considered irrevocably dead, beyond any possibility of revival. This understanding was reflected in Martha's concern about her brother Lazarus's four-day burial (see John 11:39).

Jesus' body remained in the tomb long enough to remove any doubt about the reality of his death. His body not yet decaying, but on the verge of decay, precisely fulfilled the prophecy in Psalm 16:10 that God's faithful one would not see decay.

The chief priests and Pharisees even requested guards at the tomb "until the third day" (Matthew 27:64), ensuring the security of his corpse during this time. There was zero doubt: Jesus was dead and in the grave.

And then came the resurrection—not a resuscitation, not a spiritual vision, not a metaphorical "living on in memory," but a bodily resurrection with a transformed physical existence that would never again be subject to death. As Jesus himself declared, "I am the Living One; I was dead, and now look, I am alive for ever and ever!" (Revelation 1:18).

Jesus fulfills both requirements of the Messiah: He died, satisfying the prophecies of the Suffering Servant, and he lives forever, satisfying the expectation of an eternal King. The resurrection is the ultimate validation of his messianic identity.

THE RESURRECTION AS CORONATION

When we reduce the resurrection to a promise that only applies to our future life in heaven, and eventually in the new creation, we miss the significance of this event as marking Jesus' coronation as King. This is why Peter, in his Pentecost sermon, linked the resurrection directly to Jesus' enthronement: "Fellow Israelites, I can tell you confidently that the patriarch David died and was buried, and his tomb is here to this day. But he was a prophet and knew that God had promised him on oath that he would place one of his descendants on his throne. Seeing what was to come, he spoke of the resurrection of the Messiah, that he was not abandoned to the realm of the dead, nor did his body see decay. God has raised this Jesus to life, and we are all witnesses of it" (Acts 2:29-32). For Peter, the resurrection wasn't just about the afterlife. It was about kingship. It was the fulfillment of God's promise to put a son of David on the throne forever.

Paul makes the same connection in his sermon at Antioch: "We tell you the good news: What God promised our ancestors he has fulfilled for us, their children, by raising up Jesus. As it is written in the second Psalm: 'You are my son; today I have become your father'" (Acts 13:32-33). Notice the Scripture Paul quotes: Psalm 2, a royal psalm about the enthronement of God's king. By connecting the resurrection to this psalm, Paul was declaring that Jesus' resurrection marked his coronation as the messianic King.

This explains why the earliest Christian confession wasn't "Jesus died for my sins" but "Jesus is Lord" (Romans 10:9). Jesus' death, resurrection, and ascension weren't just about securing our personal salvation; they were about establishing Jesus' universal kingship. Paul declared that because of Jesus' death and resurrection, "God exalted him to the highest place and gave him the name that is above every name, that at the name of Jesus every knee should bow, in heaven and on earth and under the earth, and every tongue acknowledge that Jesus Christ is Lord, to the glory of God the Father" (Philippians 2:9-11).

Without the resurrection, Jesus' talk about the Kingdom would be empty rhetoric. His death would represent the triumph of the kingdoms of this world over God's Kingdom. The resurrection declares that the crucified one is, paradoxically, the conquering King.

THE RESURRECTION THROUGH A WEIRD LENS

While acknowledging the legitimate personal significance of the resurrection, we must also recognize how our Western individualism can narrow its scope. In our WEIRD cultural context (see chapter 5), we can become so focused on what the resurrection means for us individually that we lose sight of its broader significance.

This individualistic focus is evident in how we typically present the gospel: "Jesus died and rose again so you can go to heaven when you die." While this framing contains truth, it reduces a cosmic event to a personal benefit package. It minimizes a declaration of Jesus' kingship over all creation into a guarantee of individual afterlife.

Even our Easter celebrations reflect this individualization. Instead of hearing messages about God's desire to redeem creation and build his Kingdom through the church, we talk about "living in resurrection power" and "claiming our resurrection victory," making the resurrection primarily about our personal spiritual empowerment rather than Jesus' enthronement as King.

In our therapeutic culture, we may also metaphorize the resurrection, turning it into a symbol for experiencing personal renewal, overcoming obstacles, or finding a new beginning. While these applications have validity, when they're the only focus, they obscure the historical reality and cosmic significance of the resurrection.

The problem with these WEIRD interpretations is not that they're false but that they're incomplete. They emphasize personal spiritual benefits while inadvertently downplaying what the resurrection says about who Jesus is and what his reign means for all creation. A balanced understanding embraces both the personal and the cosmic dimensions of the resurrection, seeing them not as competing but as complementary truths.

THE KINGDOM NOW

Beyond reshaping our understanding of the resurrection as it relates to the past and future, our WEIRD lens also obscures its implications for the present. In the church today, we may accept the resurrection as a past event (Jesus was raised from the dead) or a future promise (we will be raised from the dead), but we struggle with its present significance: Jesus reigns now.

Before his ascension, the resurrected Jesus declared, "All authority in heaven and on earth has been given to me" (Matthew 28:18). Not "will be given," but "has been given." The resurrection established Jesus' authority not just in heaven but on earth—not just in the future but in the present.

This means that the Kingdom that Jesus proclaimed has indeed arrived, though it's not yet in its fullness. His resurrection wasn't just a promise of future glory but the inauguration of present rule. This "already/not yet" tension of the Kingdom explains why Jesus taught us to pray, "Your kingdom come, your will be done, on earth as it is in heaven" (Matthew 6:10). The resurrection ensures that this prayer will ultimately be answered in full, while also empowering us to participate in its partial fulfillment now.

When we restrict the meaning of the resurrection to a promise of a future heaven, we miss its radical implications for our present on earth. The resurrection declares that Jesus is Lord—not just of our personal lives, not just of the church, but of every sphere of human existence: politics, economics, education, arts, sciences, and more. No domain is outside his authority; no area of life is exempt from his reign.

And because Jesus reigns now, we can bring our most personal concerns to him with confidence. Because his authority extends over all creation, no area of our lives is beyond his care or outside his redemptive work. Because he conquered death, we can face our greatest fears with his power at work within us. The "already/not yet" nature of his Kingdom means that while we still experience suffering, grief, and struggle, we never face those things without the presence and power of the risen King.

LIVING UNDER THE RESURRECTED KING

Since the resurrection established Jesus as the reigning King, how should this transform our lives? Let me suggest several implications that balance both the cosmic and the personal dimensions of the resurrection.

Personal Savior and Universal Lord

The resurrection challenges us to not only embrace a personal relationship with Jesus but also recognize his universal lordship.

While Jesus indeed saves individuals, he does so as the King who claims authority over all creation. We express our devotion and gratitude to him as Savior and Lord—for his grace and justice, as well as for his forgiveness and sovereignty.

As I've grown in my understanding of Jesus holding both these titles, I've found that my personal relationship with Jesus hasn't diminished; it's deepened. When I recognize that the one who knows me by name and loves me personally is also the King of kings, my relationship with him takes on greater depth and significance. I'm not just relating to a personal spiritual guide but to the sovereign Lord of all creation, who has chosen to know and love me intimately.

Future Hope and Present Reality

While the resurrection gives us hope for the future, it also establishes a present reality. Jesus reigns *now*. His Kingdom operates *now*. We're called to live under his authority in our present instead of just waiting for a future heaven.

Because Jesus reigns now, we can be confident that his promises about the future will be fulfilled too. The resurrection power we experience in part now—through transformed lives and in moments of spiritual victory—points to the full resurrection life we will experience in the age to come.

Private Faith and Public Witness

Recognizing that the resurrection declared Jesus as King, our response can't be limited to private devotion. Kings expect public allegiance, which means our faith must move from the private sphere of personal spirituality to the public sphere of visible witness. We testify not just that "Jesus died for me" but that "Jesus is Lord of all."

This public dimension doesn't replace personal transformation; it flows from it. As we experience the resurrection power of Jesus changing us from within, we naturally become witnesses to his lordship in our families, our workplaces, and our communities.

Inner Renewal and the Restoration of Creation

The resurrection points toward the renewal of all creation, not just individual lives. As Paul writes, "The creation itself will be liberated from its bondage to decay and brought into the freedom and glory of the children of God" (Romans 8:21). Our mission includes participating in this broader restoration, caring for the Kingdom as those who serve its rightful King.

This cosmic restoration doesn't replace personal renewal; it happens in conjunction with it. The same resurrection power that will one day transform creation is at work in us now—renewing our minds, healing our wounds, and conforming us to the image of Christ.

Comforting Faith and Revolutionary Allegiance

The resurrection calls us from comfortable religion to revolutionary allegiance. The powers of this world crucified Jesus precisely because his Kingdom threatened the status quo. The resurrection gave authority to his Kingdom instead of theirs. To follow the resurrected King is to pledge allegiance to his Kingdom above all other kingdoms, which will inevitably make waves and disrupt our own comfort.

Yet within this revolutionary allegiance, we find genuine comfort—not the false comfort of a domesticated Jesus who makes no demands but the true comfort of knowing that the King who calls us to follow him has conquered death itself. As Jesus told his disciples, "In this world you will have trouble. But take heart! I have overcome the world" (John 16:33). The resurrection doesn't guarantee comfort instead of challenge; rather, it promises comfort in the midst of challenge.

When we recover a true understanding of the resurrection, we begin to recover the true Jesus—not the personalized savior of WEIRD culture, but the revolutionary King who has established his throne through his death and resurrection.

This Jesus doesn't exist primarily to meet our personal needs or secure our individual afterlife. He reigns as King over all creation, calling all people everywhere to submit to his authority. He doesn't fit neatly into our personalized spirituality or privatized faith. He demands total allegiance as the resurrected and enthroned Messiah.

Don't misunderstand: This King is also intimately personal. He knows each of us by name. He invites us into relationship with him. He promises us eternal life. He offers us resurrection power for daily living. He comforts us in our grief with the assurance that death is not the end. He gives meaning to our suffering by guaranteeing that pain does not get the final word.

The question isn't just "Do you believe Jesus rose from the dead?" but "Will you submit to the authority of the resurrected King?" The issue at hand isn't simply "Do you want to go to heaven when you die?" but "Will you live under the reign of heaven now?" It's not just "Do you want the benefits of the resurrection?" but "Will you give your allegiance to the resurrected one?"

The resurrection forces a decision: Will we cling to our customized, comfortable Jesus, or will we pledge allegiance to the vindicated Messiah, the enthroned King whose resurrection changed everything?

MOVEMENT 3

10

FROM FAN TO FOLLOWER

I walked into a class called "The Life of Christ" in my second year of seminary feeling pretty confident. After all, I'd grown up in church, attended Christian schools, and won countless sword drills in youth group. I knew the Christmas story, the parables, Jesus' miracles, and the resurrection account. I could discuss theological concepts like hypostatic union and debate the nuances of Christology. If there was a pop quiz on Jesus trivia, I could crush it.

After the first day of class, I went back to my dorm room and spread the syllabus across my desk. Page after page of required reading stretched before me—not just the Gospels, but commentaries, theological works, and historical studies. I calculated the reading load: roughly a hundred pages per week. I was approaching the class as a student trying to get my mind around all the content I needed to learn and process.

By the second week, I was beginning to think that my professor had a different agenda entirely. He wasn't primarily interested in filling our heads with more information about Jesus. He was determined to transform how we approached Jesus altogether. I found myself walking out of class thinking less about what I was learning and more about how I was living.

When we studied Jesus touching the leper, he didn't just ask us about the theological significance of ritual purity laws. He asked us, "Who are the 'lepers' in your community? The people society considers untouchable? When was the last time you had a meaningful conversation with someone most people avoid?"

When we learned about Jesus' conversation with the woman at the well, he challenged us to think about our own prejudices: "What groups of people do you instinctively look down on? How do your social circles reflect or contradict Jesus' radical inclusion?"

When we read about Jesus' teachings on money, he didn't let us rationalize them as merely metaphorical. He asked pointed questions: "What does your bank statement say about your priorities? If someone examined your spending patterns, would they conclude that you follow Jesus or the American dream?"

When we studied the rich young ruler, he challenged us to consider what we might be unwilling to give up for the sake of following Jesus.

When he taught us what Jesus said about prayer and fasting, he didn't just explain the historical and theological context—he also invited us to his house for an all-night prayer meeting. Suddenly, Jesus' teachings about prayer weren't just academic concepts to analyze but spiritual disciplines to practice.

When we read about Jesus eating with tax collectors and sinners, he asked us to examine our dinner invitation lists.

When we studied Jesus' response to criticism from religious leaders, he challenged us to consider how we handle criticism of our own faith.

When we encountered Jesus' teachings about forgiveness, he didn't just expound on the theology, he asked us to identify the people in our lives we needed to forgive.

He had a way of making every Gospel story personal.

Over the course of that semester, I began to understand that there's a massive difference between studying Jesus and following Jesus. That class put me on a journey of confronting an uncomfortable truth: It's entirely possible to become an expert on Jesus while remaining a practical stranger to his way of life. We can master Christian doctrine, excel in biblical exegesis, and even enter professional ministry without truly following him. My professor wasn't just teaching us to analyze the life of Christ; he was teaching us to live the life of Christ.

Years later, I'm grateful for a professor who understood that there's a difference between studying the Messiah and following the Messiah, between academic exercise and true discipleship. The class was called "The Life of Christ," but what I really learned was how to make Christ my life.[1]

THE RABBI-DISCIPLE RELATIONSHIP

To understand what it means to make Jesus our Rabbi, we need to recover the first-century context of discipleship that our WEIRD culture has largely lost. Why does this matter? Because if we misunderstand what it means to be Jesus' disciple, we'll settle for being his fan instead. And fans might know a lot about Jesus, but they never actually become like him. The rabbi-disciple relationship is the key to transformation—it's how followers of Jesus are formed, not just informed. Our Western, individualistic culture has distorted discipleship in several key ways.

We've *privatized* discipleship. We think of discipleship as primarily a personal, individual journey rather than a communal apprenticeship. Yet Jesus called disciples into community. He sent them out in pairs. He taught them to pray "Our Father," not "My Father." We'll unpack this more in the next chapter, but true apprenticeship to Jesus happens in the context of a community of fellow apprentices.

We've *spiritualized* discipleship. We've separated spiritual formation from practical life, as if Jesus only cares about our prayer lives and Bible study. Yet Jesus' teachings address every aspect of human existence. Discipleship includes how we handle money, treat employees, engage in politics, interact with our friends and family members, and care for creation.

We've *academicized* discipleship. We've turned discipleship into an educational program focused on accumulating biblical knowledge rather than character formation. While learning is important, the goal isn't information but transformation.

We've *consumerized* discipleship. We approach discipleship by asking "What's in it for me?" rather than "How can I serve the King?" We want the benefits of following Jesus without the costs, the comfort without the cross.

In Jesus' day, a rabbi wasn't just a teacher who dispensed

information; he was a master craftsman who trained apprentices in a way of life.

The Hebrew word for *disciple* (*talmid*) literally means "learner," but it carried connotations far beyond academic study. A disciple was an apprentice who learned not just by listening to lectures but by imitating everything about his rabbi's life. The goal wasn't to accumulate knowledge but to become like the master. Their service was their lesson plan.

True discipleship operates more like a trade apprenticeship than a university education. I think of my friend Jake, who decided he wanted to become an electrician. He spent two years studying electrical theory in community college, memorizing formulas and passing tests. But when he graduated and tried to find work, he quickly discovered that knowing about electricity isn't the same as being an electrician. He needed an apprenticeship.

For the next four years, Jake worked alongside master electrician Rodriguez, watching how he diagnosed problems, learning his techniques for running wire, observing how he interacted with customers, and gradually developing the instincts that only come from walking alongside a mentor. Jake didn't just learn Rodriguez's trade; he absorbed his work ethic, his problem-solving approach, and even his way of talking to frustrated homeowners. By the time Jake earned his electrician's license, people said he worked just like Rodriguez.

If we switched from Jake and Rodriguez to you and Jesus, would your friends and family say that about you? Would they say you work just like Jesus? That you treat people like he does?

That you diagnose problems and come up with solutions in a way that reminds them of Jesus?

This is how rabbi-disciple relationships functioned in Jesus' day. The relationship was intensely personal. Disciples didn't just study their rabbi's teachings; they observed how he ate, how he prayed, how he treated his family, how he handled money, how he responded to criticism, and how he interacted with both the powerful and the powerless. Nothing about the rabbi's life was considered irrelevant to the disciple's formation.

This understanding makes Jesus' invitation more radical than we recognize. When he said, "Follow me," he wasn't recruiting students for a religious studies program. He was calling apprentices into Kingdom living. He was inviting them to pattern their entire existence after his. His closest followers understood this.

John writes, "Whoever claims to live in him must live as Jesus did" (1 John 2:6). Paul declares, "Follow my example, as I follow the example of Christ" (1 Corinthians 11:1). Peter reminds believers that "Christ suffered for you, leaving you an example, that you should follow in his steps" (1 Peter 2:21). In the Bible, "Follow me" means "Imitate me."

THE DIFFERENCE BETWEEN BELIEVING AND FOLLOWING

In our culture, we have somehow created a scenario where "believing in Jesus" doesn't necessarily involve "following Jesus"—something that would have been incomprehensible to first-century disciples. We've too often reduced faith to intellectual assent about who Jesus is or emotional experiences involving him rather than genuinely following him.

The language we use to describe our faith shows this reduction. While phrases like "accepting Jesus as our personal Savior" contain important truth, they make it sound as if Jesus is a product we can purchase as part of our spiritual inventory. I remember hearing this song for children: "If I had a little white box to put my Jesus in . . ." The problem is that Jesus is too big to fit into any box we could try to put him in.

Similarly, when we speak of "asking Jesus into our hearts," we risk reducing faith to primarily an internal, emotional experience rather than the comprehensive reorientation of life that Jesus calls for.

We can "believe in Jesus" on Sundays and, during the rest of the week, conduct our business, politics, and relationships according to entirely different principles. We've compartmentalized Jesus into the spiritual aspect of our lives while keeping him out of other areas. This distinction would have been foreign to Jesus' first disciples, who understood that following the Messiah meant bringing every aspect of life under his authority.

Picture your life as a dresser with multiple drawers. One drawer is labeled "Money." It contains your financial decisions, spending habits, and career choices. Another drawer says "Entertainment." It's filled with your movie preferences, music choices, and social media habits. There's a "Work" drawer that holds your professional ambition and who you are on the job. You have a "Relationships" drawer containing how you handle conflict, forgiveness, and love. There's a "Politics" drawer, a "Sexuality" drawer, and so on—each one representing a different area of your life.

Then there's the "Jesus" drawer. It's usually organized and tidy, filled with Bible verses, church attendance, prayer time, and religious vocabulary. We keep this drawer separate from the others, pulling it out on Sundays or holidays or times of crisis, then carefully closing it when we move on to "real life."

As a pastor, I feel this compartmentalization acutely when I preach. If I try to open someone's "Money" drawer during a sermon, talking about generosity, debt, or materialism, I see people's faces change. Their body language says, "Hey, that's not the 'Jesus' drawer. Stay in your lane, Preacher." If I address the "Entertainment" drawer by challenging what we watch or how we spend our leisure time, I get pushback: "Keep my Saturday night out of your Sunday-morning sermons. That's personal. That has nothing to do with my faith." Or, if the protest is more "spiritual," they may say, "I live by grace, not law."

If I dare to open the "Politics" drawer and suggest that following Jesus might challenge some of our political assumptions, the tension in the room becomes palpable. People want Jesus to bless their political views, not question them. The "Sexuality" drawer is often completely off-limits for people who have convinced themselves that what we do with our bodies has nothing to do with our faith. Other people would prefer to think Jesus didn't delve into the topic at all.

But here's what Jesus is calling us to: He doesn't want to be a drawer in your dresser; he wants to be the entire dresser. He doesn't want a compartment of your life; he wants to transform every compartment. When Jesus calls us to follow him, he's not asking for access to one area of our lives; he's asking to redesign the entire piece of furniture.

The first disciples understood this. When Matthew left his tax booth, he wasn't just adding a "Jesus" drawer to his life. He was letting Jesus transform his "Money" drawer, his "Career" drawer, and his "Identity" drawer (see Matthew 9:9). When Zacchaeus encountered Jesus, he immediately opened his home, his table, and his friend circle. His "Wealth" drawer spilled out everywhere when he promised to give half his possessions to the poor and make restitution to those he'd cheated (see Luke 19:1-10).

This is why making Jesus our Rabbi is so threatening to our comfortable Christianity. A rabbi doesn't just influence the spiritual part of your life; he redesigns your entire life. He teaches you how to think about money, how to treat people, how to approach work, how to handle conflict, how to view entertainment, and how to engage in politics. From the bedroom to the boardroom, nothing is off-limits to his teaching and authority.

The compartmentalized Jesus seems safe because he's manageable. We can open that drawer when we need comfort, guidance, or forgiveness, then close it when his teachings become inconvenient. But Rabbi Jesus is dangerous because he demands access to everything. He wants to transform not just what you pray for but what you pay for. Not just how you worship but how you work. Not just how you believe but how you live in every area of your life.

This is what we've been missing. When we encounter the true Messiah—not just a personalized Savior but the revolutionary King who demands total allegiance—transformation is inevitable. The disciples' radical life changes weren't optional add-ons to their faith; they were the natural result of recognizing who Jesus really is. Their transformed lives became evidence of an accurate understanding of the Messiah. We cannot truly encounter the King of kings and remain unchanged.

INVITING JESUS INTO YOUR WHOLE LIFE

The missing Messiah we've been recovering throughout this book isn't missing because he's hard to find; he's missing because we've confined him to a single drawer. Perhaps that's why eternal life *now* eludes us. He can't bring eternal life into places we don't allow him to go.

Compartmentalizing Jesus is a real struggle. It's a struggle for churches; it's a struggle in our own hearts. Here are some examples from conversations I've had over the last few weeks.

I met Sarah after church one Sunday. As a marketing executive who considers herself a devoted Christian, she leads Bible studies, volunteers at church events, and can quote Scripture with ease. Yet she confessed that her job requires her to create advertisements that she knows prey on people's insecurities and promote a kind of materialism she doesn't believe in. "I compartmentalize it," she explained. "My faith is my personal relationship with Jesus, but my career is just how I make a living." Sarah has bought into a version of Christianity that allows her to worship Jesus on Sunday while spending Monday through Friday being discipled by our culture. Her work feeds the cultural obsession with image and consumption—values that Jesus consistently challenged. There are no simple solutions to complex situations like this, but I have to wonder what it would look like for her to bring Jesus' values into her daily work. Admittedly, there might be awkward conversations and potential fallout, but it could also open opportunities for God to be active in her work life. The question is clear: Is Jesus King or merely Savior?

Mike is a committed church member who tithes faithfully and serves on multiple committees. He genuinely loves Jesus and can articulate the gospel clearly. But when it comes to his neighborhood, he admitted he has never had a meaningful conversation with his Muslim neighbors because, as he put it, "I just don't know what we'd have in common." He regularly expresses concern over "those people" moving into the area and changing the community. Mike believes deeply in Jesus' love for all people but hasn't allowed that belief to shape how he treats the "others" in his daily life. When he pulls into his driveway after church, his faith is more theoretical than transformational. He has "Samaritans" next door who might be open to the good news, if only he would talk to them.

Jennifer describes herself as a "Jesus follower" who is passionate about worship and prayer. She attends every church service and conference, seeking what she calls "deeper spiritual experiences." Yet she acknowledged that she has been estranged from her sister for three years over a family dispute, and she has no intention of reaching out for reconciliation. "That's different," she insisted. "You don't know how hurt I was. Some things are unforgivable." Jennifer has embraced a spirituality that seeks intimacy with God while refusing to practice the forgiveness that Jesus made central to following him. She wants the emotional benefits of faith without its relational demands. She isn't willing to imitate Jesus by praying, "Father forgive them." While not every relationship can or should be reconciled, every wrong can and should be forgiven, as Christ forgave us (see Ephesians 4:32).

When the Messiah is our King, his forgiveness flows through us, and that's our best chance to be reconciled with others.

David is a passionate Christian who can defend his faith intellectually and speak passionately about social justice issues. He regularly posts about caring for the poor, and he criticizes churches that he feels are too focused on comfort. But when I asked him about his own giving patterns, he was defensive, admitting that he donated less than one percent of his income to charity because he was "building wealth for the future" and wanted to be financially secure first. David has developed a faith that is prophetically vocal about others' responsibilities but conveniently silent about his own. He has turned following Jesus into a theoretical position rather than a practical commitment. He missed the Messiah's model of prioritizing the poor. I can't help but wonder how his perspective about the poor would broaden if he were to experience firsthand the joy of giving his own time, resources, and money to those in need.

In our individualistic culture, we've created what Dallas Willard criticized as a "gospel of sin management," a version of faith that focuses only on forgiveness of sins and assurance of heaven without demanding earthly allegiance.[2] We offer people eternal life without requiring them to actually follow Jesus in this life. We've separated salvation from discipleship—as if it were possible to truly know Jesus without becoming like Jesus.

FAN VERSUS FOLLOWER

About a decade ago, I was having coffee with a recent college graduate who had grown up in our church. As we caught up, he mentioned that he and his girlfriend had just moved in together.

"I know what you're thinking," he said quickly, "but we're planning to get married eventually. And honestly, it just makes financial sense right now, with student loans and everything."

I asked him how he reconciled this with following Jesus.

"Look, I still believe in Jesus," he replied. "I still pray and read my Bible sometimes. This is just . . . different. It's about practical life decisions, and culturally, a lot has changed since the Bible was written."

Sitting there, I realized he had perfectly illustrated the difference between being a fan of Jesus and truly following him.

Here's the most basic definition of a fan: "an enthusiastic admirer."

It's the guy who goes to the football game with no shirt and a painted chest, cheering from the stands. He has a signed jersey hanging on his wall and multiple bumper stickers on his car. But he's not in the game. He never breaks a sweat or takes a hard hit. He knows all about the players and can rattle off their stats, but he doesn't really know the players. He yells and cheers, but nothing is required of him. There's no sacrifice he has to make.

It's the woman who never misses the celebrity news shows and is constantly on the TMZ website. She's a huge fan of a certain actress and knows everything about her—what high school she attended, her birthday, her first boyfriend's name, even her real hair color. She knows everything there is to know about this actress, but she doesn't really know her. She's an enthusiastic admirer.

I think Jesus has a lot of fans these days. Fans who root for him when things are going well but walk away when life gets difficult. Fans who sit safely in the stands cheering but know nothing of the sacrifice and pain required on the field. Fans who know all about him but don't actually know him.

Jesus has never been interested in having fans. When he defines what kind of relationship he wants, "enthusiastic admirer" isn't an option. As I look at the trends in Christianity over the past few decades, my concern is that instead of being training centers for disciples, our churches are stadiums full of fans. Every week, people come to cheer for Jesus, but are they really following him? They want to be close enough to Jesus to get all the benefits but not so close that anything is required from them.

THE NEW TESTAMENT'S CLASSIC FAN

In John 3, we meet a fan named Nicodemus. He wasn't just any fan; he had box seats! He was a well-known and well-respected religious leader, a member of the Sanhedrin. He had been an admirer of Jesus for some time, inspired by his teaching and amazed by his miracles.

Nicodemus was ready to take his relationship with Jesus to a deeper level, but it wasn't easy. There was much to lose if he went public as a follower of Jesus. What would people think if they found out that this respected religious leader had made this homeless carpenter his rabbi? At the very least, he would lose his position and reputation. Being a secret admirer of Jesus cost him nothing, but becoming a follower came with a high price tag. It always does.

The story tells us something crucial about Nicodemus's approach: "He came to Jesus at night" (John 3:2). Why at night? He had plenty of opportunities during the day, when Jesus was teaching publicly. Given his position, people would have stepped aside to let him speak with Jesus. But he came at night.

At night, no one would see him. At night, he could avoid awkward questions from other religious leaders. At night, he could spend time with Jesus without anyone else knowing. Maybe he could begin a relationship with Jesus without having to make any real changes. He could follow Jesus without it impacting his job or disrupting his comfortable life.

That sounds like a lot of fans I know. They want to follow Jesus as long as it doesn't require any significant changes or have any negative implications. We read about Nicodemus two more times in Scripture. In John 7, he speaks up for Jesus before the Sanhedrin itself. He is immediately silenced by their rebuke. The final time we meet him is in John 19:38-42, when he helps Joseph of Arimathea put Jesus in the grave. We can't know for sure where Nicodemus stood in his view of the Messiah, but I have to wonder if he held back from following him fully because of his fear of what his peers would say or what it would mean for his reputation. Regardless, don't you want to be more than Jesus' mortician? He's not calling you to care for his remains. He's calling you to follow him.

Here's the reality: There's no way to follow Jesus without having him interfere with your life. Following Jesus always costs something. For Nicodemus, it likely would have cost him his powerful position, the respect of his colleagues, his source of income, his friendships, and likely some family relationships.

This brings up a telling question for most fans: Has following Jesus cost you anything? I don't mean that to be rhetorical.

Take a moment and honestly consider: What has following Jesus really cost you? How has being his apprentice interfered with your life? Would it be too strong of a statement to say that if following Jesus isn't costing you anything, you're doing it wrong?

Jesus himself said that following him included denying yourself and taking up a cross (see Luke 9:23). Most of us don't mind Jesus making minor changes in our lives, but Jesus wants to turn our lives upside down. Fans don't mind having him do a little touch-up work, but Jesus is looking to do a complete renovation. Fans come to Jesus thinking *tune-up*, but Jesus is thinking *overhaul.* Fans think a little makeup is fine, but Jesus is thinking makeover. Fans want Jesus to inspire them, but Jesus wants to interfere with their lives. Fans purchase tickets; followers are sold out.

In John 3, Nicodemus begins his conversation by making it clear that he believes Jesus is from God. He came to a point of belief, but where did he go from there? He had made a decision about believing in Jesus, but that's not the same as following him. Jesus didn't just want Nicodemus at night; he wanted him during the day. Jesus isn't looking for a relationship based solely on belief; he wants people who will follow him.

Jesus warned about those who claim allegiance to him without following him: "Not everyone who says to me, 'Lord, Lord,' will enter the kingdom of heaven, but only the one who does the will of my Father who is in heaven. Many will say to me on that day, 'Lord, Lord, did we not prophesy in your name and in your name drive out demons and in your name perform many miracles?' Then I will tell them plainly, 'I never knew you. Away from me, you evildoers!'" (Matthew 7:21-23).

This passage is sobering because it describes people who seem religious and even perform miracles in Jesus' name, yet Jesus says he never knew them. The issue isn't their lack of supernatural activity but their lack of authentic relationship.

This warning should prompt us to examine our own relationship with Jesus. Have we created a form of Christian faith that knows a great deal about Jesus but doesn't actually follow him?

The danger of false discipleship is that it can feel spiritual while requiring very little actual change. We can attend church, listen to worship music, and slap a Christian bumper sticker on our car while never submitting our lives to Jesus' authority.

PRACTICAL APPRENTICESHIP

So what does it look like to make Jesus our Rabbi, in practical terms? Let me suggest several dimensions of authentic apprenticeship.

Know Him, Not Just His Teaching

Jesus defined eternal life as knowing God through him (see John 17:3). When we think of the word *knowing*, we naturally connect it to the word *knowledge*. But biblical "knowing" involves much more than intellectual understanding or comprehension. It includes intimate experience and participation.

The Hebrew word *yada* is often used to suggest not just knowledge but the deepest possible intimacy, the kind of knowing that comes only through relationship. It's the same word used to describe the intimate knowledge between husband and wife. You can study everything about someone—their biography, their preferences, their history—but until you actually spend time with them, experience life together, and develop a relationship, you don't truly know them. Here is a simple litmus test: Could you finish Jesus' sentences like you do with your best friend?

As we know him, we become more like him. Don't mistake that for perfect performance or sinless living. Even Jesus' original disciples failed regularly—and, at times, massively. Peter denied him, Thomas doubted him, and the sons of Zebedee misunderstood his Kingdom. What made them disciples wasn't their perfection but their commitment to knowing and following Jesus. The same is true for us: When we walk closely with him through the ups and downs of life, we start to talk like him, think like him, act like him, and love like him.

Practice His Priorities

To get a feel for what was important to Jesus, we can take a look at a two-day period in his ministry, recorded in Mark 1:21-39. On the Sabbath, he taught in the synagogue, then immediately went to care for Simon Peter's sick mother-in-law. That evening, he healed many who were brought to him. Early the next morning, while it was still dark, he went to a solitary place to pray. When the disciples found him, he said, "Let us go somewhere else—to the nearby villages—so I can preach there also. That is why I have come" (verse 38).

Over the span of just two days, Jesus' priorities are clear: spending time with his Father, caring for the marginalized, telling the truth, and staying committed to his mission. If you're following Jesus, his priorities should be reflected in your priorities. Scour the past two days of your own life, looking at your schedule, your budget, your relationships, and your goals. Do they align with the priorities of your Rabbi?

Embrace His Mission

Jesus came to establish God's Kingdom on earth. Making him your Rabbi means joining this mission, not figuring out how you can benefit from it. When we pray, "Your kingdom come, your will be done, on earth as it is in heaven" (Matthew 6:10), we're not just asking God to do something; we're volunteering to answer our own prayer.

Think about what we're asking for when we pray this prayer. We're asking for God's justice to come to earth, which means we need to be willing to work for justice. We're asking for God's peace to come to earth, which means we need to be peacemakers. We're asking for God's love to be demonstrated on earth, which means we need to love others sacrificially. We're asking for God's mercy to be shown on earth, which means we need to be merciful.

Every time we pray, "Your kingdom come," we're essentially saying, "God, use me to bring heaven to earth."

Develop His Character

Character formation happens through intentional practice. Let's take two of Jesus' core character traits: compassion and humility.

Compassion is the most common emotion ascribed to Jesus in the Gospels. Again and again, we read that he was "moved with compassion"—for the crowds, his friends, the sick, the grieving, the lost. Yet here's the irony: When we know all about Jesus without actually knowing Jesus, we often become less compassionate, not more. We become experts in theology but strangers to the heart of the one we study. We can quote verses about God's love while showing little love ourselves.

The way to develop the compassion of Jesus is through practice. Start small—notice the person everyone else ignores. Pray and ask God to give you the eyes of Jesus for the hurting. Practice seeing people the way Jesus sees them: not as interruptions to your agenda but as image-bearers deserving dignity and care.

Humility is equally central to Jesus' character. He says, "Learn from me, for I am gentle and humble in heart" (Matthew 11:29). Yet when our faith becomes academic rather than relational, or when we're focused more on dogma than on listening, we tend toward pride, not character transformation. We become self-righteous—more interested in being right than in showing Jesus' love.

Humility grows through recognizing our dependence on God and others. It develops when we admit our need for correction, when we serve without seeking recognition, when we choose others' interests over our own. Jesus, who had every right to demand service, instead served others. His apprentices must learn to do the same.

Submit to His Authority

The heart of discipleship is submitting to Jesus' authority in every arena of life. This means allowing his teachings to shape your business practices, political views, spending patterns, and relationship choices, even when it's costly or countercultural.

There's an ancient Jewish saying (paraphrased): "May you be covered in the dust of your rabbi." It refers to disciples who follow their rabbi so closely that they're literally covered in the dust kicked up by his feet as he walks. The image suggests proximity and commitment—you go wherever he goes, following closely at whatever pace he sets, regardless of the terrain or the obstacles.

That image is inspiring and poetic, but in practical terms, what does it mean? Here are a few ideas of what it looks like to be "covered in the dust" of Rabbi Jesus:

- Follow his teaching on forgiveness, even when you've been deeply hurt.
- Practice his generosity, even when it affects your financial security.
- Embrace his inclusivity, even when it makes others uncomfortable.
- Pursue his purpose, even when it costs you socially or professionally.
- Live by his sexual ethics, even when culture rolls its eyes.
- Show his compassion, even to those who might hurt you.

When we're covered in his dust, we become recognizable as his disciples. People see Jesus in us not because we're perfect but because we're authentically and intentionally following in his footsteps.

DYING DAILY

Jesus was honest about the cost of discipleship: "Whoever wants to be my disciple must deny themselves and take up their cross daily and follow me" (Luke 9:23). Making Jesus our Rabbi isn't about adding religious activities; it's about dying to ourselves.

Paul makes this declaration in 1 Corinthians 15:31, writing, "I die daily" (KJV). While Paul was facing physical harm as a result of persecution, even believers whose lives aren't being threatened face a similar struggle: The hardest part of carrying your cross and dying to yourself is that it's so . . . *daily*.

This death is more literal than you might think. It involves dying to our need to be right, our desire for comfort, our pursuit of status, and our illusion of control. It means allowing Jesus' priorities to override our preferences, his mission to redirect our ambitions, and his way of life to transform our habits.

But here's the irony: This kind of death leads to resurrection. Jesus promised, "Whoever loses their life for me will find it" (Matthew 16:25). In dying to our false selves, we discover our true selves—the people God created us to be. In submitting to Jesus' authority, we find genuine freedom. In embracing his mission, we finally discover deep and fulfilling purpose.

11

FOLLOWING JESUS TOGETHER

A few years ago, I was having coffee with a successful entrepreneur who had been attending our church sporadically. And by sporadically, I mean he had come twice. I was challenging him about making church a higher priority, and he was almost immediately defensive.

"I love Jesus, but I'm not really into the whole church thing. Going to church doesn't make me a Christian. My relationship with Jesus is personal."

I'm sure a friend or family member has said something like this to you before: "I can follow Jesus without the church." Or, "I love Jesus. I just don't like the church." It doesn't just sound reasonable; it sounds spiritual. Who needs organized religion when you can have a pure, unmediated relationship with God?

As I sat across from this entrepreneur, it struck me that he was inadvertently illustrating one of the most dangerous misconceptions in contemporary Christianity: the idea that following Jesus is primarily an individual endeavor. But this idea isn't just unbiblical; it's impossible. You can't fully follow Jesus solo because Jesus didn't design discipleship to work that way.

It's like the cymbal player who insists they can master their craft by practicing alone in their garage. They can learn the basic techniques, study the music, and even develop perfect timing with a metronome. But cymbals without an orchestra are just noise. The beauty and purpose of cymbals—the very reason they exist—is to accentuate the crescendo, to punctuate the climax, to add drama to the symphony. A cymbal player who refuses to join the orchestra will never experience what their instrument was designed for. They might become technically proficient, but the magic happens when the instruments come together.

The previous chapter challenged us to move from knowing about Jesus to really knowing him—not as students but as apprentices. That's what it means to make him our Rabbi. Here's what our individualistic culture doesn't want to hear: We can't make Jesus our Rabbi while rejecting his body, the church. Biblical discipleship is inherently communal. To follow Jesus as Messiah is to become part of his revolutionary community.

In first-century Judaism, rabbis didn't train disciples one-on-one. They gathered a group of *talmidim*, or disciples, who learned not just from the rabbi but from each other. The *talmidim* would debate the rabbi's teachings together, challenge one another's understanding, and sharpen their interpretations through group discussion. They didn't just follow the rabbi as isolated individuals; they followed him as a learning community.

The relationship was inherently communal because the rabbis understood something we've forgotten: We can't fully comprehend and apply truth in isolation. The *talmidim* needed each other to see what they couldn't see alone, to ask questions they wouldn't think to ask, and to apply the rabbi's teachings in ways that might not occur to them individually.

In my own decades of discipling, I can attest that students learn as much from each other as from their mentor.

A few years ago, I was meeting weekly with a small group of guys: Marcus, a new Christian; Jake, a lifelong church kid wrestling with doubt; and Tom, a businessman trying to integrate faith and work.

One morning, Marcus shared that he was struggling to forgive his absent father. Before I could offer my pastoral wisdom, Jake spoke up. "Man, I get that. My dad was there physically but checked out emotionally. I spent years hating him for it." Then he told Marcus about choosing to forgive his dad—not because his dad deserved it, but because he was becoming bitter. "Forgiveness didn't heal my dad," Jake said, "but it healed me."

Marcus sat there, nodding slowly. Later, he told me that Jake's story hit him harder than anything I could have said.

That's how the rabbi-disciple model is supposed to work. The rabbi forms a community of learners who sharpen one another and multiply what they're learning together.

When Jesus called his disciples, he didn't call Peter, James, John, and the others to separate, private relationships with himself. He called them into a community that learned together, failed together, grew together, and ultimately transformed the world together.

Please hear me: This chapter isn't just about church attendance or small group participation or checking religious boxes. In fact, attending church can be isolating. If someone shows up at church occasionally, faces forward, and leaves without connecting or conversing with anyone, not much community is happening there. But when the church is functioning as Jesus intended, it acts as the contemporary incarnation of the Messiah on earth. Please don't miss this. I'll shout if I have to: The body of Christ is the continuing incarnation of Jesus the Messiah. That's something no one can do alone. We aren't just individuals who happen to believe similar things about Jesus. Together, we are the body of Christ, the living presence of the revolutionary King in the world today.

THE FAMILY OF GOD

From the very beginning, following Jesus was understood to mean joining a community, becoming part of an interdependent group, entering a new family. It was such an obvious part of following Jesus that it was assumed.

Jesus made this family dynamic explicit in one of the most radical statements he ever made. When his mother and brothers came looking for him while he was teaching, someone told him, "Your mother and brothers are standing outside, wanting to speak to you."

Jesus' response was shocking: "Who is my mother, and who are my brothers?" Then, pointing to his disciples, he declared, "Here are my mother and my brothers. For whoever does the will of my Father in heaven is my brother and sister and mother" (Matthew 12:46-50).

Jesus wasn't being disrespectful or minimizing the value of family. This was his way of announcing that following him creates a new kind of family bond. The community of disciples wasn't just an educational arrangement or a temporary association. It was a family, bound together not by blood or law but by shared allegiance to the Father and commitment to Jesus as Messiah.

Throughout the Gospels, we see how Jesus emphasized the communal nature of following him.

When he sent the disciples out, he sent them in pairs (see Luke 10:1).

When he taught them to pray, he gave them plural pronouns: "*Our* Father" (Matthew 6:9, emphasis added).

When he described his followers, he used collective metaphors: "You [plural] are the salt of the earth"; "You [plural] are the light of the world" (Matthew 5:13, 14).

When he promised his presence, it was in the context of community: "Where two or three gather in my name, there am I with them" (Matthew 18:20).

When he established Communion, he said, "Do this in remembrance of me." He instituted a communal meal, not individual meditation (1 Corinthians 11:23-26).

When he promised the Holy Spirit, he said, "You will receive power," using the plural *you*, indicating that the Spirit was given to the community collectively (Acts 1:8).

THE BODY OF CHRIST

Paul's letters make the communal nature of faith even more explicit. He wasn't writing to isolated individuals but to communities. His primary metaphor for the church is a body: one organism with many parts, each dependent on the others (see 1 Corinthians 12:12-27). For Paul, the idea of a solitary Christian would be as absurd as a detached hand trying to function without the rest of the body.

Think about it: A severed hand might still look like a hand, but it can't do what hands are designed to do. It can't feel, grip, create, or serve. Without the circulation system, the nervous system, the skeletal structure, and the muscular support of the whole body, a hand is just dead tissue. It maintains the appearance of a hand while lacking all the function of a hand.

This is Paul's point about Christians who are trying to go it alone. You might maintain the appearance of faith—you can still read your Bible, pray, and hold theological opinions. But as we will see, you lose the essential functions that faith was designed for. Without the body, individual faith becomes spiritually lifeless, no matter how sincere it appears. Paul drives this point home when he says, "The eye cannot say to the hand, 'I don't need you!' And the head cannot say to the feet, 'I don't need you!'" (1 Corinthians 12:21).

Paul's metaphor of the church as the body of Christ is more than a nice illustration; it's a theological reality with practical implications. We are not *like* a body; we *are* the body of Christ on earth today. This means that when the church gathers, Jesus is present—not just spiritually, but corporately. We become his hands, his feet, his voice, and his heart in the world.

This incarnational understanding of the church should radically transform how we think about gathering with other believers. We're not just getting together to sing songs, hear a sermon, and go home. We're not just gathering to get our spiritual needs met or even to learn more about Jesus. We're coming together to be the body of Christ to one another and to the world.

I've watched this reality unfold as our church has begun meeting in addiction recovery centers on Sunday mornings. At first, some people wondered, "Why would we meet there? Isn't church supposed to happen in a church building?" But that question reveals a misunderstanding of what the church really is. The church isn't a building—it's the people. And when the people of God show up in places where people are fighting for their lives, the body of Christ is made manifest.

When we gather in recovery centers, something remarkable happens. The people in recovery see that the church isn't just inviting them to come to us—we're going to them. We're saying, "You don't have to get cleaned up to meet Jesus. We'll bring Jesus right here, into the middle of your struggle." Our presence says that no place is too broken for the body of Christ to inhabit. And as we worship together, pray together, and share Communion together in those spaces, we're not just talking about Jesus' love for the marginalized—we're embodying it.

This is what it means to be the body of Christ. We don't just point people to Jesus; we follow Jesus next to them through our collective life together.

THE COST OF GOING IT ALONE

As I was telling my friend about the priority of community, he pushed back. "Look, I hear what you're saying about community being ideal, but my current approach is working fine for me. I read my Bible, I pray before my meals, I try to live by Christian principles. The way I do it seems to be working."

I paused, choosing my words carefully. "Can I ask you something? How do you know it's working?"

He seemed surprised by the question. "Well, I feel closer to God. I understand the Bible better than I used to. I'm becoming a better person."

"But here's the thing," I said gently. "You're comparing your current experience to your past experience or to no faith experience at all. You've never actually experienced what it's like to follow Jesus in authentic community. It's like someone who has only had a black-and-white TV telling me that it works fine. The individualistic approach does work, to a point. It works until it doesn't. And compared to what Jesus had in mind, it doesn't get close. Even if it works for you, it doesn't work for those you could 'work' for. You aren't contributing to the health of the body where you could—and should. The value of community isn't merely what you get out of it but what you invest in it."

He frowned. "That seems a bit harsh."

"I don't mean it to be harsh," I replied.

What I wanted to say but didn't is this: Because we live in such an individualistic culture, it can be hard for us to diagnose the symptoms of individualistic faith. Like a fish that doesn't notice the water it swims in, we've become so accustomed to privatized religion that we can't see how it's affecting our spiritual health. We mistake independence for maturity, isolation for intimacy with God, and self-reliance for spiritual strength.

Since that conversation, I've thought more about the consequences of trying to follow Jesus outside authentic community. Here are some of the potential pitfalls to consider:

We'll Lack Spiritual Endurance

Following Jesus requires perseverance through seasons of doubt, disappointment, and spiritual dryness. Without a community to encourage us, challenge us, and carry us through difficult times, we're likely to give up when faith gets hard. The Christian life is a marathon, not a sprint, and marathons aren't meant to be run alone. This is why the writer of Hebrews makes community a command: "Let us not neglect our meeting together, as some people do, but encourage one another" (Hebrews 10:25, NLT).

In what ways have you been cheered on by others in the journey of faith? Who have you encouraged to persevere?

We'll Become Spiritually Self-Deceived

Without the accountability and honest feedback that comes from authentic community, we'll justify our compromises, rationalize our sin, and lose the ability to see our own blind spots. We are all capable of self-deception, and we need people who love us enough to tell us the truth about ourselves.

Paul recognized this, as evidenced by his admonition to believers: "Speaking the truth in love, we will grow to become in every respect the mature body of him who is the head, that is, Christ" (Ephesians 4:15). Notice that spiritual maturity happens when we speak truth to each other in love. It's a community function, not an individual achievement. Without others who will lovingly confront our blind spots, we remain spiritually immature, no matter how much we study or pray on our own.

Can you think of a time when someone spoke the truth to you in love? How did it feel in the moment? How do you see it now, with the advantage of hindsight?

We'll Develop Theological Blind Spots

Our understanding of Scripture is filtered through our cultural context and personal biases. Left on our own, we'll miss how the gospel speaks to people of different classes, ages, races, perspectives, and life experiences. Every book of the Bible was written to a community and intended to be understood and applied in the context of community.

Think back on times you've read Scripture with people from different backgrounds. What insights or new perspectives have you learned from these believers?

We'll Struggle with Accountability

Without others who know our struggles and ask us the hard questions, we'll find it easier to compromise in private areas of our lives. Hidden sins like pride, lust, greed, and bitterness will grow unchecked because there's no one with permission to call them out. Of course, the Holy Spirit can convict us of sins, but he frequently does so through the people we're in community with.

James explains how this works: "Confess your sins to each other and pray for each other so that you may be healed" (James 5:16). Notice that healing from sin happens through confession to one another—not just privately in prayer, but to trusted members of the community. Without this kind of vulnerable accountability, our secret struggles tend to remain in darkness and hold power over us.

Have you ever experienced healing as a result of confessing your sins to someone else—whether that healing was physical, emotional, or spiritual?

We'll Miss Our Full Purpose

God has given us specific gifts meant to serve others in the body of Christ. Without community, these gifts remain dormant and undeveloped. We'll live below our spiritual potential because we're not using our gifts for their intended purpose.

Paul makes this clear: "To each one the manifestation of the Spirit is given for the common good" (1 Corinthians 12:7). Notice that spiritual gifts are given not for personal benefit but for the common good. They're designed to function in community. A gift that's not used to serve others is like a muscle that atrophies from lack of use. Without the body of Christ to serve, our God-given abilities remain undiscovered and underdeveloped.

What gifts do you have that seem to be dormant right now? How might God be prompting you to use those gifts to benefit the body of Christ?

We'll Become Spiritually Stagnant

Growth happens through relationship and challenge. Without others to sharpen us (see Proverbs 27:17), encourage us to take risks, and push us beyond our comfort zone, our spiritual life will plateau and eventually decline.

If your spiritual life were a body of water, what would you compare it to right now? An ocean? A flowing river? A stagnant pond? A puddle? Is there something that needs to change in your life to bring vibrancy to your faith?

We Won't Fully Know Jesus

Here's a truth that might make you feel uncomfortable, and by uncomfortable, I mean offended: You cannot fully know Jesus by yourself. We need the eyes of the community to see who he really is. You can see the fingerprints of God in nature, but his full portrait is found in the body of Christ.

If we're trying to follow Jesus alone, we'll inevitably develop a Jesus who looks suspiciously like us—sharing our personality, our political views, our cultural blind spots, and our personal preferences. Without the corrective lens of community, our understanding of Jesus will be limited by our own perspective and experiences.

When you picture Jesus, what does he look like? What does he sound like? What does he talk about? What about him makes you uncomfortable? Whose perspective might you be missing to see a fuller picture of who he is?

A REFLECTION OF JESUS

Jesus is described in Scripture with dozens of metaphors and titles. He's the Good Shepherd, the Bread of Life, the Light of the World, the Door, the Way, the Truth, the Life, the Alpha and the Omega, the Prince of Peace, the Lion of Judah, the Lamb of God, the High Priest, the King of kings, and so much more.

No individual will fully experience all these dimensions of who Jesus is. But in community, we begin to see his fullness.

I know Jesus as Healer in a deeper way because I've watched him work through the nurses and doctors in our congregation during medical crises. I know him as Provider because I've seen how our community mobilizes to meet one another's needs during unemployment or financial hardships. I know him as Challenger because other believers have confronted me when I've settled for less than his best. I know him as Comforter because I've witnessed how his presence shows up through the embrace of other followers during times of grief.

John, a member of our congregation, is a physician who sat by the bedside of his dying adult son. His son had walked some difficult roads, including drug addiction and suicidal ideation. By God's grace, he'd come back home and come back to church. Not long after that, he had a medical episode that shut down his body. In order for his organs to be donated, he was kept on life support long after hope was gone. For several days, John sat with his son's nonresponsive body. When they finally took him off life support, John heard God's voice: "I have your son, and you have mine." Nothing took away the pain of losing his son, but this loss has also had a redemptive arc. Whenever anyone in our church loses a child, you know who shows up? John.

Each member of the body reflects different aspects of Jesus' character. The mercy giver shows us his compassion. The justice seeker reveals his righteousness. The generous giver displays his sacrificial love. The truth teller demonstrates his honesty. The peacemaker embodies his reconciling Spirit. Together, we form a more complete picture of who Jesus is than any of us could create alone.

This is why Paul says the church is "the fullness of him who fills everything in every way" (Ephesians 1:23). We are not just individuals who happen to follow Jesus; we are collectively the fullness of Christ on earth. When we're functioning as we should, the watching world will be able to look at our community and see Jesus.

I remember hearing about a pastor whose father was deeply skeptical of Christianity and the church. Whenever the pastor would invite his dad to visit, his father would wave him off with the same dismissive comment: "All the church wants is another name and another dollar. Just somebody else to count and another dollar for the offering plate."

Years went by with the father refusing every invitation to church. Then he was diagnosed with throat cancer. After serious surgery that left him unable to speak, he wasted away in the hospital until he was just seventy-four pounds.

Even though this man had spent years criticizing the church and refusing to have anything to do with it, something unexpected happened. Church members started showing up. Not for him—they barely knew him. They came for his son, the pastor, who had been there for them through their own difficult times.

They brought cards, flowers, and food for the family. They sat with the pastor during long hospital vigils. They surrounded this skeptical man with the very community he'd spent years dismissing.

During one of his father's final days, the pastor sat by his hospital bed reading aloud the cards that church members had sent. His father, unable to speak, wrote something on a piece of paper and handed it to his son. It said simply, "I was wrong."

The father had discovered what my entrepreneur friend was struggling to understand: We really do need one another. The community he had dismissed as just wanting another name and another dollar had shown him what the body of Christ looks like when it functions the way Jesus intended.

A REVOLUTIONARY COMMUNITY

My entrepreneur friend didn't seem convinced by the case I was making for gathering as a community of believers. I pressed forward, trying to be respectful while also getting my point across. "Let me tell you what you're missing," I said with a gentle smile. "When you say you can follow Jesus without the church, you're not just opting out of religious services. You're rejecting the very plan Jesus implemented."

He looked skeptical. I couldn't blame him—he had attended church a few times but had never experienced a community of believers who understood the messiahship of Jesus. I tried to explain, "What I'm talking about isn't just a religious organization or a spiritual social club."

I described to him the early church we read about in Acts 2:42-47. They shared their possessions so no one was in need. They broke bread together daily, not just on Sundays. They prayed together, learned together, and served together. Rich and poor, slave and free, Jew and Gentile sat at the same table as equals. This was so radical that it turned the world upside down (see Acts 17:6).

This revolutionary community didn't happen by accident. It was the direct result of believers recognizing Jesus as the Messiah. When Peter preached on Pentecost and three thousand people responded, they didn't just accept Jesus as their personal Savior; they joined a movement, entered a community, and became part of the body.

Churches that miss the Messiah tend to operate as religious service providers and focus almost exclusively on an individual's salvation, personal spiritual growth, and private relationship with God.

Churches that recognize the Messiah, however, understand that they are called to embody the Kingdom of God on earth. These are incarnational communities that operate as the body of Christ.

After talking with my friend about this, he was quiet for a moment. Then he asked, "But what does that really look like?"

As I looked at him, I thought about a story I once heard about a young preacher in a southern Tennessee town. On his first Easter Sunday, he discovered that the church he was serving had an unusual tradition. Every Easter, in the afternoon, all the church members went to a lake, where they baptized people. Two little tents were set up where people could change clothes and dry off. Later in the evening, after the baptisms, they would build a fire, and they would sing a few songs. Then they'd gather in a circle, with the new Christians in the center. One by one, the people would go around the circle and introduce themselves to the new members.

They would say, "Hi. My name is . . . If you ever need any ironing or washing done, I'd be glad to help you!" "My name is

. . . If you ever need anybody to drive you to the grocery store or the doctor, you can call me." "My name is . . . If you ever need anybody to babysit, I'd sure be glad to help you." "My name is . . . I can work on cars. So if you're ever having any trouble with your car, I'll do some mechanical work for you." "My name is . . . I'm a plumber. If you ever have any trouble in that way, feel free to give me a call."

And so it would go, all around the circle. They would sing another song or two, and then they would eat and play games. Finally, after it was dark, one of the deacons would say, "Well, folks, it's time to go home."

This young preacher said that the first year, he hung around after everyone had gone. The only person left was the deacon who had said it was time to go home. He was over at the fire pit, kicking out the fire with his size 13s. The deacon said to the preacher, "Well, preacher, it doesn't get any better than this. People don't get much closer than this. They've got a name for what you were a part of tonight. It's called church."

Most churches focus on getting people ready for heaven. But Jesus' mission was about bringing heaven to earth. When Jesus taught his disciples to pray, he didn't say, "Help us get to your Kingdom." He said, "Your kingdom come, your will be done, on earth as it is in heaven" (Matthew 6:10). The goal isn't simply to evacuate earth for heaven; it's to invade earth with heaven.

Instead of just asking, "How do we get more people to heaven?" we ask, "How do we bring more of heaven here?"

Instead of just seeing the church as a refuge from the world, we see it as God's agent for transforming the world.

Instead of primarily measuring success by attendance,

budget, or baptisms, we measure success by how well we're faithfully embodying Kingdom values.

As my conversation with my entrepreneur friend wound down, it was becoming glaringly obvious that the kind of community I was describing is something the church often falls short of. So I took a moment and apologized to him.

"Look, I need to be honest with you," I said, setting down my coffee cup. "I've been sitting here telling you what the church should be, but I also need to acknowledge what it often is. You've probably experienced churches that felt more like country clubs than revolutionary communities. You've probably encountered Christians who were more interested in being right than being loving. You've likely seen church leaders who seemed more concerned with building their own kingdoms than God's Kingdom. You may have even been hurt by people in the name of religion." I made it clear I wasn't just apologizing for the theoretical church; I was also confessing my part in it. More often than I want to admit, I can get caught up in Western culture's priorities and methods.

I paused, feeling the weight of conviction about what I was saying. "I'm sorry. I'm sorry that the church has so often been a disappointment rather than a demonstration of Jesus' love. I'm sorry that we've given you reasons to think you're better off without us. I'm sorry that we've made church feel like another obligation rather than the life-giving community it was meant to be."

And then I asked my friend something—something I want to humbly ask you: Would you not retreat into religious isolation but help us become the revolutionary community Jesus envisioned?

- The church was never meant to be a place where people come to be entertained but a community where people come to be equipped.
- The church was never meant to be a spiritual gas station where we fill up and drive away but a training center where we learn to live differently.
- The church was never meant to be a refuge from the world's problems but a force for solving them.
- The church was never meant to be a collection of perfect people but a hospital for broken people learning to find healing together.
- The church was never meant to be rows of people sitting passively but waves of people transforming the world.
- The church was never meant to be an institution that preserves the status quo but a movement that challenges everything that stands against God's Kingdom.

Will you help the church become what Jesus had in mind? Will you bring your gifts, your questions, your struggles, your testimony, and your dreams into community with other broken people who are trying to follow the revolutionary Messiah?

I'm not asking you to find a perfect church—that doesn't exist. I'm not asking you to ignore the church's failures—they're real, and we need Jesus to restore and redeem, and you can be part of that redemption. You are invited to help the church move from rows to waves, from institution to movement, from comfortable religion to revolutionary community. Because the church is not complete without you. And honestly? You are not fully you without the church.

AFTERWORD

BETWEEN THE BANQUETS

The first miracle of Jesus recorded in Scripture was at a wedding banquet. And the first thing Jesus will do when he returns is bring his people to a banquet—a wedding banquet, to be precise.

The initial banquet is recorded in John 2, when Jesus and his disciples attended a wedding. Scripture doesn't say anything about this, but I have a hunch that twelve thirsty men could drain a few bottles of Mogen David. Jesus' mother was keeping an eye on the food and wine at this seven-day celebration, and she came to Jesus in a panic because they had run out of wine. This would have brought shame to the groom, who was supposed to provide generously for his guests to showcase his ability to care for his bride. This faux pas also would have embarrassed Mary, as it seems to have been her responsibility to ensure the meals were properly managed.

Jesus seems to have dismissed his own mother at first. Rather than calling her "Mom," "Mother," or "Yes, ma'am," he said, "*Woman*, why do you involve me?" (John 2:4, emphasis added).

She didn't let that dissuade her. She turned to the servants and said, "Do whatever he tells you" (verse 5).

What he told them was bizarre: They were to take six stone jars and fill them with water, then deliver them to the master of ceremonies. When they did, the water miraculously turned to wine. We're not talking about a paltry amount. These stone jars would have held twenty to thirty gallons each. Do the math—that's a blessing you can bathe in!

Why is this important? Because this is the first of seven signs in John.[1] Notice that these are not simply miracles like those recorded in the other Gospels; these are also signs. What's the difference? A miracle is a supernatural act that displays God's power. A sign is a miracle that points beyond itself to reveal something about who Jesus is and what he came to do. Every sign in John's Gospel is like a flashing arrow saying, "Pay attention—this tells you something crucial about the Messiah."

Seven is a significant number in Scripture. It symbolizes God's complete work among people. Taken together, these seven signs guide us on a journey to full discipleship, ending with the resurrection of Lazarus. This final miracle previews the promise he makes to all of us: that in the end, he will raise us from the dead—with new bodies, in a new heaven and a new earth. That's when we will gather for the second wedding feast—the marriage supper of the Lamb (see Revelation 19).

What does all this mean? It means that the start of discipleship is an invitation to a celebration, which concludes with a final feast when Jesus returns. Between these two banquets, however, is what Revelation calls the great tribulation (7:14). Whether we're currently experiencing the final tribulation now,

I cannot say—and I'm not sure it really matters. The times we're living through are enough to cause tribulation for any of us. But they're bracketed by a feast.

What do followers of Jesus—those who acknowledge Jesus' role and authority—do in the in-between period?

ETERNAL LIFE NOW

The purpose of this book has been to restore our understanding of the true Messiah. To help us see him as he is, through his own words and actions. He is not just a Savior but the Messiah, the King of Israel, and the Son of God. He is identified in the New Testament as the Christ, which means "the Anointed One." However, over the course of time, this title has lost some of the original implications of the Hebrew word *Messiah*.

As we look back at Jesus' lineage and life, we see that Jesus surpasses the Jewish expectations for a Messiah, the Greek understanding of a spiritual emperor, and the boxes we ourselves put him in. He is broader, deeper, wider, and higher than we can imagine. He is Yahweh in the flesh. He is the King of kings—not only in heaven, but also here on earth. He is committed to saving our souls, for sure. But beyond that, he aims to reshape our families, our finances, our friendships, and our communities. He wants to be our Rabbi, the one we follow as apprentices. We are to live as he did, speak as he did, and focus on the matters that concerned him.

When we follow Jesus wholeheartedly like this, it means a complete reconfiguration—requiring us to change our religious systems and our personal lives. It means redistributing our resources, time, and priorities. It calls for a shift not only in our personal lives but also within our churches.

Why does this matter to us today? I think it's pretty clear that we are living in times of unprecedented change. Technology is advancing at a rate more rapid than we can keep up with, and while it promises improvement and opportunity, it also leads to complex ethical quandaries, increased mental health concerns, depersonalization, and the loss of relationship and community. There is a real risk that the technology we hope will make our lives better will turn into an idol that enslaves us.

The world is at a crossroads, and, with it, the church. At other critical junctures in history—during times of rapid change in the world—the followers of Jesus had a choice to make: Would they succumb to the values of their culture under pressure, or would they stand strong in the unchanging truth of Scripture and the unfailing character of God? We don't know exactly what challenges our world will face in the next decade, but make no mistake: Testing is coming. Will we be blown by the cultural winds, or will we stay true to the Messiah as he has been revealed to us in Scripture?

The stakes are high, just as they were in Jesus' time. He told the religious leaders, "You study the Scriptures diligently because you think that in them you have eternal life. These are the very Scriptures that testify about me, yet you refuse to come to me to have life" (John 5:39-40). The religious leaders were steeped in their religious culture, but it wasn't enough to bring them eternal life. Today, we have the gift of being on the other side of the cross, but we, too, can get stuck in our limited perspective of who Jesus is. Our religious habits and expectations can't give us eternal life either. Only Jesus can do that. Until we truly know him—not just the image we have of him, but Jesus himself—we will not fully experience eternal life as he intended—both today and forever (see John 10:10).

THE HOTTER THE FIRE . . .

Jesus told his disciples to rejoice in suffering: "Blessed are you when people insult you, persecute you and falsely say all kinds of evil against you because of me. Rejoice and be glad, because great is your reward in heaven, for in the same way they persecuted the prophets who were before you" (Matthew 5:11-12).

By fully knowing Jesus and relentlessly following him, you will experience eternal life today. That doesn't mean you'll face fewer trials and tribulations; you will likely face more. But part of experiencing eternal life involves allowing God to develop Christ's character in you through suffering.

When an object is under pressure, it will do one of two things: break or become stronger. Circumstances themselves aren't solely responsible for destroying something, but they do reveal what it's made of. Certain things, like diamonds, can be strengthened under pressure. The same can be true for Christians.

When Peter and John were arrested by the Sanhedrin, the pressure caused them to rise to the occasion (see Acts 4). They stood boldly before the religious elite and put them on notice that their preaching of Jesus was nonnegotiable. The leaders were stunned by the disciples' bold faith. They realized that these humble fishermen had been with Jesus. Later, when the apostles were physically assaulted, they returned to the other believers, rejoicing because they had been deemed worthy to suffer for the name of Jesus (see Acts 5). With this posture of embracing suffering for the sake of Christ, the spread of the gospel was virtually unstoppable. When persecution erupted under Saul, the opposition only emboldened them and made them more courageous (see Acts 8).

This same principle is repeated throughout the New Testament. James 1:2-4 encourages us to rejoice in our trials because they produce steadfastness. Peter reminds us that our trials refine our faith like gold in a fire (see 1 Peter 1:7). And Paul teaches that suffering produces perseverance, character, and hope (see Romans 5:3-4). Of all people on the planet, followers of the Messiah should be the most resilient, joyful, productive, and hopeful.

The higher the pressure, the stronger the diamond. The hotter the fire, the purer the gold. When the pressure comes in our lives, may we rise to the top, shining the light of Christ in the dusk of humanity.

Under the weight of a mental health crisis, followers of the Messiah model resilience, hope, and compassion. In a society fractured by political division, followers of the Messiah exalt the one true King. In a world of technological isolation, followers of the Messiah gather in person to sing, comfort, unify, and speak truth. In an economy increasingly divided by haves and have-nots, followers of the Messiah are marked by their radical generosity. In a culture of narcissistic individualism, followers of the Messiah exemplify sacrificial love to others.

Change inevitably feels scary to us mere mortals. But God has not left us to face these uncertainties alone. Not only does he invite us to know him—the long-promised and long-awaited Messiah and the King of kings—but he also promises to be with us as Immanuel. As you face challenges and testing today and in the days ahead, cling to him fiercely. Obey him radically. Pursue him relentlessly. Remember his true character. Stay rooted in community. Share his love with the world. He is with you now, providing eternal life today.

ACKNOWLEDGMENT

TO PHILIP B. SMITH:

This project has our names on it, but it didn't start with us. You are the third strand in this "cord of three," and you were its true impetus. Though readers will likely not read your words or hear your voice, you are the creative visionary, relentless encourager, and generous supporter of *The Missing Messiah*. Without you, this offering would not have come to fruition.

APPENDIX A

OLD TESTAMENT PROPHECIES ABOUT THE MESSIAH

Reference	Summary	Role	New Testament Reference
Genesis 3:15	Protoevangelium	King	Romans 16:20; Hebrews 2:14
Genesis 49:10	Shiloh prophecy	King	Matthew 2:6; Luke 1:32-33
Numbers 24:17-19	Star of Jacob	King	Matthew 2:2; Revelation 22:16
Deuteronomy 18:15-19	Prophet like Moses	Prophet	Acts 3:22-23; John 1:45
1 Samuel 2:10	Hannah's prayer	King	Luke 1:46-55
2 Samuel 7:12-16	Davidic covenant	King	Luke 1:32-33; Acts 2:30; Hebrews 1:5
1 Chronicles 17:11-14	Davidic covenant	King	Luke 1:32-33; Hebrews 1:5
Psalm 2:7-9	God's anointed King	King	Acts 4:25-26; 13:33; Hebrews 1:5; Revelation 2:27
Psalm 2:8-9	Ruling with an iron rod	King	Revelation 2:27; 12:5; 19:15
Psalm 16:10	Won't see decay	King	Acts 2:27-31; 13:35-37
Psalm 18:49	God's anointed King	King	Romans 15:9
Psalm 22	Suffering Servant	Prophet	Matthew 27:35-46; Mark 15:24-34; John 19:23-24, 28

Reference	Summary	Role	New Testament Reference
Psalm 45:6-7	Royal wedding psalm	King	Hebrews 1:8-9
Psalm 72:1-2; 8; 11; 17	Royal psalm	King	Matthew 2:11; Revelation 21:24-26
Psalm 89:3-4	Davidic covenant	King	Luke 1:32-33
Psalm 89:20-29	Davidic covenant	King	Acts 13:22-23
Psalm 110:1-4	Melchizedek	King/ Priest	Matthew 22:44; Acts 2:34-35; Hebrews 5:6; 7:17-21
Psalm 118:22-23	Cornerstone	Prophet	Matthew 21:42; Mark 12:10-11; Luke 20:17; Acts 4:11; 1 Peter 2:7
Psalm 132:11-18	Davidic covenant	King	Luke 1:32-33; Acts 2:30
Isaiah 7:14	Immanuel	Priest	Matthew 1:22-23
Isaiah 9:1-7	Mighty God	King	Matthew 4:15-16; Luke 1:32-33
Isaiah 11:1-16	Root of Jesse	King	Romans 15:12; Revelation 5:5
Isaiah 35:4-6	Healing Redeemer	Priest	Matthew 11:4-5; Luke 7:22
Isaiah 40:9-11	Shepherd King	King	John 10:11-16
Isaiah 42:1-9	Servant song	Prophet	Matthew 12:18-21
Isaiah 49:6	Servant song	King	Acts 13:47; Luke 2:32
Isaiah 50:4-11	Servant song	Prophet	Matthew 26:67; 27:30
Isaiah 52:13–53:12	Suffering Servant	Prophet	Matthew 8:17; Acts 8:32-33; 1 Peter 2:22-25
Isaiah 59:20-21	Redeemer for Zion	King	Romans 11:26-27
Isaiah 61:1-3	Anointed	King	Luke 4:18-19
Isaiah 62:11-12	Coming Savior	King	Matthew 21:5
Jeremiah 23:5-6	Righteous Branch	King	Matthew 2:2; Luke 1:32-33
Jeremiah 30:9	David	King	John 18:37; Revelation 19:16

Reference	Summary	Role	New Testament Reference
Jeremiah 31:31-34	New Covenant	Priest	Hebrews 8:8-12; 10:16-17
Jeremiah 33:14-26	Righteous Branch	King/ Priest	Luke 1:32-33; Hebrews 7:11-22
Ezekiel 34:23-24	David as shepherd	King	John 10:11-16
Ezekiel 37:24-28	David as king	King	John 10:11-16; Revelation 21:3
Daniel 7:13-14	Son of Man	King	Matthew 24:30; 26:64; Revelation 1:7; 14:14
Daniel 9:24-27	Seventy weeks	Prophet	Matthew 24:15; Mark 13:14
Hosea 3:5	Return to David	King	Luke 1:32-33
Amos 9:11-15	Tent of David restored	King	Acts 15:16-17
Micah 5:2-4	Ruler from Bethlehem	King	Matthew 2:5-6
Habakkuk 3:13	Anointed King	King	Acts 13:23
Zechariah 3:8	Branch	King	Luke 1:78
Zechariah 6:12-13	Branch as priest-king	King/ Priest	Hebrews 7:1-3
Zechariah 9:9-10	King on a donkey	King	Matthew 21:4-5; John 12:14-15
Zechariah 12:10	Pierced One	Prophet	John 19:34-37
Zechariah 13:7	Struck Shepherd	Prophet	Matthew 26:31; Mark 14:27
Malachi 3:1-5	Elijah	Prophet	Matthew 11:10; Mark 1:2

APPENDIX B

NEW TESTAMENT CITATIONS OF MESSIANIC PROPHECIES

Note that Old Testament references alluded to rather that quoted are in italics.

New Testament Reference	Old Testament Reference	Role	Topic
Matthew 1:22-23	Isaiah 7:14	Priest	Born of a virgin
Matthew 2:5-6; John 7:42	Micah 5:2-4	King	Messiah born in Bethlehem
Matthew 2:15	Hosea 11:1	King	Called out of Egypt
Matthew 2:17-18	Jeremiah 31:15	Prophet	Weeping for lost children
Matthew 3:17; Hebrews 1:5	*Psalm 2:7*	King	"You are my Son"
Matthew 4:6; Luke 4:10-11	Psalm 91:11-12	Priest	Angels protect the Chosen One
Matthew 4:15-16	Isaiah 9:1-2	King	Light to the Gentiles
Matthew 8:17	Isaiah 53:4-6	Prophet	He bore our griefs
Matthew 12:18-21	Isaiah 42:1-4	Prophet	Servant brings justice gently
Matthew 13:14-15; Mark 4:12; Luke 8:10	Isaiah 6:9-10	Prophet	Hearts hardened to truth

New Testament Reference	Old Testament Reference	Role	Topic
Matthew 13:35	Psalm 78:2	Prophet	Speaking in parables
Matthew 15:8-9; Mark 7:6-7	Isaiah 29:13-14	Prophet	Lip service without heart
Matthew 21:5; John 12:15	Zechariah 9:9	King	King comes riding a donkey
Matthew 21:9; 23:39; Mark 11:9; Luke 13:35; 19:38; John 12:13	Psalm 118:25-26	King	"Blessed is he who comes . . ."
Matthew 21:13; Mark 11:17; Luke 19:46	Isaiah 56:7	Priest	House of prayer proclaimed
Matthew 21:13; Mark 11:17; Luke 19:46	Jeremiah 7:11	Prophet	Den of thieves exposed
Matthew 21:16	Psalm 8:2	King	Praise from children's mouths
Matthew 21:42; Mark 12:10-11; Luke 20:17; Acts 4:11; 1 Peter 2:7	Psalm 118:22-24	King	Rejected stone becomes the cornerstone
Matthew 22:44; Mark 12:36; Luke 20:42-43; Acts 2:34-35	Psalm 110:1-4	King	The Lord sits at God's right hand
Matthew 24:15; Mark 13:14	Daniel 9:24-27; 11:31; 12:11	Prophet	Abomination of desolation foretold
Matthew 24:29; Mark 13:25	Isaiah 13:9-11	Prophet	Sun and moon darkened
Matthew 24:30; Mark 13:26; Luke 21:27	*Daniel 7:13-14*	King	Son of Man coming
Matthew 26:15	*Zechariah 11:12*	Prophet	Betrayed for thirty silver pieces
Matthew 26:31; Mark 14:27	Zechariah 13:7	Prophet	Shepherd struck and sheep scattered

New Testament Reference	Old Testament Reference	Role	Topic
Matthew 26:63	*Isaiah 53:7*	Prophet	Silent before his accusers
Matthew 27:9-10	*Zechariah 11:13*	Prophet	Silver thrown to the potter
Matthew 27:35; Mark 15:24; Luke 23:34; John 19:24	*Psalm 22:18*	Prophet	Garments divided by lots
Matthew 27:46; Mark 15:34	Psalm 22:1	Prophet	"My God, why have you forsaken me?"
Matthew 27:57-60	*Isaiah 53:9*	Prophet	Buried with the rich
Luke 2:32; Acts 13:47	*Isaiah 49:6*	Prophet	Light to the nations
Luke 4:18-19	Isaiah 58:6-7	King	Proclaiming captives set free
Luke 4:18-19	Isaiah 61:1-2	Prophet	Spirit anoints Jesus to preach
Luke 22:37	Isaiah 53:10-12	Prophet	Numbered with the transgressors
Luke 23:46	Psalm 31:5	Prophet	Jesus' spirit committed to Father
John 1:10-11	*Isaiah 53:3*	Prophet	Rejected by his own
John 1:45; 6:14	*Deuteronomy 18:15-19*	Prophet	Prophet like Moses promised
John 1:51	Genesis 28:12	Priest	Heaven opening; angels ascending
John 2:17	Psalm 69:9	Prophet	Zeal for God's house consumes Jesus
John 6:31-35	Exodus 16:4	Priest	Bread from heaven given
John 6:45	Isaiah 54:13	Prophet	All taught by God
John 10:34-36	Psalm 82:6	King	"You are gods" declared
John 12:38; Romans 10:16	Isaiah 53:1	Prophet	People do not believe his message

New Testament Reference	Old Testament Reference	Role	Topic
John 12:40; Acts 28:26-27	Isaiah 6:9-10	Prophet	God blinded their eyes
John 13:18; Matthew 26:24	Psalm 41:9	Prophet	Friend betrayed him
John 15:25	Psalms 35:19; 69:4	Prophet	Hated without cause
John 19:36	Exodus 12:46	Prophet	No bones broken
John 19:37	Zechariah 12:10	Prophet	They look on the one pierced
Acts 2:16-21	Joel 2:28-32	Prophet	Spirit poured on all
Acts 2:25-28	Psalm 16:8-11	Priest	Not abandoned to the realm of the dead
Acts 3:22-23; 7:37	Deuteronomy 18:15-19	Prophet	Prophet like Moses
Acts 3:25	Genesis 12:1-3	King	Numerous descendants
Acts 4:25-26	Psalm 2:1-2	King	Nations rage against the Anointed
Acts 7:6-7; Romans 4:18	Genesis 15:5-14	King	Descendants like stars
Acts 8:32-33	Isaiah 53:7-8	Prophet	Led as lamb to the slaughter
Acts 13:33	Psalm 2:7	King	"You are my Son"
Acts 13:34	Isaiah 55:3	King	Everlasting covenant of David
Acts 13:35	Psalm 16:8-11	Priest	Holy One won't see decay
Acts 13:41	Habakkuk 1:5	Priest	Wonders people won't believe
Acts 15:16-17	Amos 9:11-12	King	David's tent restored
Romans 1:17; Galatians 3:11; Hebrews 10:37-38	Habakkuk 2:4	Prophet	Righteous will live by faith
Romans 9:9	Genesis 18:10-18	King	Sarah will have a son

New Testament Reference	Old Testament Reference	Role	Topic
Romans 9:25; 1 Peter 2:10	Hosea 2:23	King	"I will call them 'my people'"
Romans 9:26	Hosea 1:10	King	Children of the living God
Romans 9:33	Isaiah 8:14-15	Prophet	Stone of stumbling placed
Romans 9:33; 10:11; 1 Peter 2:6	Isaiah 28:16	King	Cornerstone in Zion laid
Romans 10:6-8	Deuteronomy 30:11-14	Prophet	The Word is near you
Romans 10:13	Joel 2:28-32	Prophet	All who call will be saved
Romans 10:15	Isaiah 52:7-11	King	Beautiful feet bringing news
Romans 10:19	Deuteronomy 32:21	Prophet	Provoked by foolish nation
Romans 11:8	Isaiah 29:10	Prophet	Spirit of stupor given
Romans 11:26-27	Isaiah 59:20-21	King	Redeemer comes to Zion
Romans 11:34	Isaiah 40:13	Prophet	Who knows the Lord's mind?
Romans 14:11; Philippians 2:10-11	Isaiah 45:23	King	Every knee shall bow
Romans 15:3	Psalm 69:9	Prophet	Insults about God fall on Jesus
Romans 15:9	2 Samuel 22:50-51	King	Praise among the Gentiles
Romans 15:10; Hebrews 1:6	Deuteronomy 32:43	Prophet	Gentiles rejoice with God's people
Romans 15:11	Psalm 117:1	King	Praise among the Gentiles
Romans 15:12	Isaiah 11:10	King	Root of Jesse arises
1 Corinthians 2:9	Isaiah 64:4	Priest	No eye has seen God's plan

New Testament Reference	Old Testament Reference	Role	Topic
1 Corinthians 2:16	Isaiah 40:13	Prophet	"Who has known God's mind?"
1 Corinthians 3:20	Psalm 94:11	Prophet	Lord knows thoughts are vain
1 Corinthians 15:27	Psalm 8:4-6	King	All is under his feet
1 Corinthians 15:45-49	Genesis 2:7	Priest	First man, living soul
1 Corinthians 15:54	Isaiah 25:8	Priest	Death swallowed in victory
1 Corinthians 15:55	Hosea 13:14	Priest	"Death, where is your sting?"
2 Corinthians 4:6	Genesis 1:3	Priest	Light shines from darkness
2 Corinthians 6:16	Ezekiel 37:26-28	King	God walks with his people
Galatians 3:6-8	Genesis 15:5-14	King	Abraham's seed blesses all nations
Galatians 3:8, 16	Genesis 12:7; 13:15	King	Single seed promised
Galatians 3:13	Deuteronomy 21:23	Prophet	Cursed are those on a tree
Ephesians 4:8	Psalm 68:18	King	He ascended on high
Hebrews 1:5; 5:5	Psalm 2:7; 2 Samuel 7:14	King	"You are my Son"
Hebrews 1:8	Psalm 45:6-7	King	His throne is forever
Hebrews 1:13; 5:6; 7:17, 21	Psalm 110:1-4	Priest/King	Sit at my right hand
Hebrews 2:6-8	Psalm 8:4-6	King	Son of Man is honored
Hebrews 2:12	Psalm 22:22	Prophet	Praise in the assembly
Hebrews 2:13	Isaiah 8:17-18	Prophet	The children given to him
Hebrews 3:2, 5	Numbers 12:7	Prophet	Prophet like Moses

New Testament Reference	Old Testament Reference	Role	Topic
Hebrews 3:7-15	Psalm 95:7-11	Priest	"Do not harden your hearts"
Hebrews 4:4	Genesis 2:2	Priest	God's Sabbath
Hebrews 8:5	Exodus 25:40	Priest	Everything made by plan
Hebrews 8:8-12; 10:16-17	Jeremiah 31:31-34	Priest	New covenant
Hebrews 9:19-20	Exodus 24:8	Priest	Blood of the covenant
Hebrews 10:5-10	Psalm 40:6-8	Priest	He doesn't desire sacrifices
Hebrews 12:26	Haggai 2:6	Prophet	He will shake the heavens
1 Peter 1:24-25	Isaiah 40:6-8	Prophet	The Word of God lasts
1 Peter 2:8	Isaiah 8:14-15	Prophet	Stone causes stumbling
1 Peter 2:22-23	Isaiah 53:9	Prophet	He committed no sin
1 Peter 2:24-25	Isaiah 53:4-6	Prophet	By his wounds we're healed
Revelation 1:7	Zechariah 12:10; Daniel 7:13	Prophet	He comes with the clouds
Revelation 2:27; 12:5; 19:15	Psalm 2:9	King	Rules with an iron scepter
Revelation 5:5	*Isaiah 11:1*	King	Root of David
Revelation 7:17; 21:4	Isaiah 25:8	Priest	Tears wiped away
Revelation 14:14	Daniel 7:13-14	King	Son of Man on the clouds
Revelation 15:3-4	Psalm 111:2-3	King	Psalm of the Lamb
Revelation 15:3-4	Jeremiah 10:7	King	Psalm of praise
Revelation 15:4	Psalm 86:9; 98:2	King	Psalm of praise

APPENDIX C

PROPHET, PRIEST, AND KING

In appendix A and appendix B, we examined Scripture to determine whether the passages describe the Messiah mainly as a king, a priest, or a prophet. Admittedly, this isn't an exact science but more like shades on a color wheel. The portrait that emerges shows some interesting tones. Check out this chart and see what you notice:

Source	Total	King	Prophet	Priest	Percentage
Old Testament Prophecies (appendix A)	51	70%	24%	6%	100%
Jewish Literature*	63	43%	43%	14%	100%
New Testament Cites Old Testament (appendix B)	153	41%	43%	16%	100%
"Christ" in New Testament†	534	85%	4%	6%	95%

* See MissingMessiah.com.
† See MissingMessiah.com.

Notice how the numbers keep multiplying faster than loaves and fishes. Those fifty-one original Old Testament prophecies? They're just the appetizer. The New Testament triples that number and then—hold on to your scrolls—triples it again when counting uses of *Christ*. Here's a mind-bender for you: The Gospels use the word *Christ* only a fraction of the time Paul does (54 times compared to 382 times). It was as if the title Christ was reserved until after he proved it through the resurrection. Eagle-eyed readers might notice these percentages only add up to 95 percent in the last row. What happened to the other 5 percent? That 5 percent falls into a brand-new category: "Son of God" (see appendix D).

APPENDIX D

SON OF GOD

Here is a summary of times the title *Son of God* is used in the New Testament and when it is used.

Who Said It	Where	With Christ	What	When‡
Gabriel	Luke 1:35		Annunciation to Mary	6 BC
John the Baptist	John 1:34		Testimony about Jesus	AD 30
Nathanael	John 1:49		Confession of Jesus	AD 30
Satan	Matthew 4:3, 6; Luke 4:3, 9		Temptations of Jesus	AD 30
Demon-possessed man	Matthew 8:29; Mark 5:7; Luke 8:28		Jesus' encounter with Legion (Mark and Luke add "Most High")	AD 30
Demons	Mark 3:11; Luke 4:41	X	Jesus' ministry in Capernaum	AD 31
Jesus	John 5:25		Jesus claims to be an eschatological judge	AD 32
Disciples	Matthew 14:33		After Jesus walked on water	AD 32
Peter	Matthew 16:16	X	Great confession	AD 32

‡ Note that scholars differ on these dates.

Who Said It	Where	With Christ	What	When§
Jesus	John 10:36		Teaching on Psalm 82:6	AD 32
Jesus	John 11:4		Raising of Lazarus	AD 33
Martha	John 11:27	X	Raising of Lazarus	AD 33
Caiaphas and the Jewish leaders	Matthew 26:63; Luke 22:70; John 19:7	X	Jesus' trial	AD 33
Crowds	Matthew 27:40, 43		Crucifixion	AD 33
Centurion	Matthew 27:54; Mark 15:39		Crucifixion	AD 33
Paul	Acts 9:20		Saul's conversion	AD 38
Mark	Mark 1:1	X	Intro to the Gospel	AD 48
Paul	Galatians 2:20	X	Paul's life statement	AD 50
Paul	2 Corinthians 1:19	X	Intro to the Epistle	AD 56
Paul	Romans 1:4	X	Intro to the Epistle	AD 57
Paul	Ephesians 4:13	X	Statement on the body of Christ	AD 60
Luke	Luke 3:38		Genealogy in reference to Adam (where Jesus is the new Adam)	AD 62
Author of Hebrews	Hebrews 4:14; 6:6; 7:3; 10:29		Theological argument	AD 65
John	John 3:18		Narrative description of Jesus	AD 92
John	John 20:31	X	Purpose of the Gospel	AD 92
John	1 John 3:8; 4:15; 5:5, 10, 12, 13, 20	X	Theological argument	AD 93
Jesus	Revelation 2:18		Letters to the seven churches	AD 95

§ Note that scholars differ on these dates.

APPENDIX E

JESUS' FULFILLMENT OF HIS PREDECESSOR ELIJAH

Miracle/Event	Elijah	Jesus
Raising the dead	Widow's son in Zarephath (1 Kings 17:17-24)	Widow's son at Nain (Luke 7:11-17)
Multiplying food	Flour and oil for the widow (1 Kings 17:8-16)	Food for 5,000 (Mark 6:30-44)
Controlling rain	Called for a drought (1 Kings 17:1; 18:41-45)	Calmed the storm (Mark 4:35-41)
Calling fire from heaven	Called down fire on soldiers (2 Kings 1:1-18)	Refused to call down fire on the Samaritans (Luke 9:54-55)
Confronting rulers	King Ahab and Jezebel (1 Kings 18)	King Herod and Pilate (Luke 23)
Crossing water	Parted the Jordan River (2 Kings 2:8)	Walked on the Sea of Galilee (John 6:19)
Ascending	Taken to heaven in a whirlwind (2 Kings 2:11)	Ascended to heaven (Acts 1:9-11)

APPENDIX F

JESUS' FULFILLMENT OF OLD TESTAMENT PREDECESSORS

Hero	Virtue	God's Call	Jesus' Fulfillment
Adam	Innocence	Adam was created in the image of God and called to reproduce life on earth. But his disobedience ended innocence and brought death (Genesis 3:6).	Jesus is the new Adam, ending death (Romans 5:17-19) and being made perfect through obedience (Hebrews 5:8-9).
Abraham	Faith	Abraham was the father of the faithful by leaving country and kin to create a new nation (Genesis 15:6; Romans 4:3; Galatians 3:6; Hebrews 11:8-9; James 2:23).	Jesus is the author and perfector of our faith (Hebrews 12:2), who left his Father in heaven, creating a new nation.
Jacob	Persistence	Originally, Jacob "supplanter" was known for deception and cunning. Later, he is known as Israel—"One who wrestles with God" (Genesis 25:26; 32:28). He was tasked to be the father of twelve tribes.	Jesus had no deceit or sin (1 Peter 2:22). He didn't wrestle with God; he submitted to him (Luke 22:42). He called twelve disciples to follow him, mirroring the dispersed tribes.

Hero	Virtue	God's Call	Jesus' Fulfillment
Moses	Humility	Moses was known as the most humble man (Numbers 12:3), yet in a fit of self-aggrandizement, he struck the rock for water rather than speaking to it (Numbers 20:8-12). For that, he was disallowed to enter the Promised Land.	Jesus was the ultimate model of humility (Philippians 2:5-11) and was exalted because of it, leading us into our true Promised Land (Hebrews 3:16–4:11).
David	Heart	Though David was a man after God's own heart (1 Samuel 13:14; Acts 13:22), he numbered his troops, trusting his own strength rather than God's (2 Samuel 24). Because of all his bloodshed, he was not allowed to build the Temple for God (1 Chronicles 22:8).	Jesus, in contrast, rules his Kingdom in full obedience, trust, and submission to God (John 5:30; 6:38; Hebrews 10:7). Jesus also shed his own blood as the foundation stone for building a new temple (Matthew 21:42).
Solomon	Wisdom	Solomon wrote an entire book of wisdom, yet his son Rehoboam single-handedly destroyed the unity of the kingdom. He shows that you can be wise without modeling wisdom.	Jesus, in contrast, is the wisdom from God (1 Corinthians 1:24) and gives us the Spirit of wisdom so we have the mind of Christ (1 Corinthians 2:6-16) and empowerment for ministry (Acts 4:13; Colossians 1:28).
Elijah	Zeal	Elijah, after defeating 450 prophets of Baal, fell apart, fleeing from Jezebel (1 Kings 19:4, 10). He lamented that he alone was left, when he knew that Obadiah hid one hundred prophets in a cave (1 Kings 18:13) and God claimed to have seven thousand who had not bowed the knee to Baal (1 Kings 19:18).	Zeal for God's house consumed Jesus (John 2:17). Rather than fleeing from danger, he marched resolutely to the cross. Jesus defeated principalities and powers (Colossians 2:15), even when he was truly abandoned by his closest followers (Matthew 26:31-32, 56; John 16:32).

NOTES

CHAPTER 1: WHO DO YOU SAY JESUS IS?

1. "Excerpt from 'The Message of God,'" Experiencing History: Holocaust Sources in Context, accessed November 20, 2025, https://perspectives.ushmm.org/item/excerpt-from-the-message-of-god.

CHAPTER 2: CHRIST IS *NOT* JESUS' LAST NAME

1. Beyond 2 Samuel 7 and Psalm 2, a constellation of words orbits around this mystic figure. (1) There are regal words, such as *star* (see Numbers 24:17), *scepter* (see Genesis 49:10; Psalm 45:6; 110:2), *horn* (see 1 Samuel 2:10; Psalm 132:17), *crown* (see Psalm 132:18), *throne* (see 2 Samuel 7:13, 16; Psalm 89:4, 29; 132:11-12; Isaiah 9:7), and a bunch of talk about a *kingdom*. (2) There are words about his genealogy, both metaphorical—*branch, root, shoot,* and *stump* (see Isaiah 11:1; 53:2; Jeremiah 23:5; 33:15; Zechariah 3:8; 6:12)—and literal—*firstborn*, *begotten*, and *son* (see 2 Samuel 7:14; Psalm 2:7, KJV, 12; 72:1; 89:27; Isaiah 7:14; 9:6; Zechariah 12:10). (3) There are words describing his leadership roles, like *ruler* (see Genesis 49:10; Numbers 24:19; Daniel 9:25; Micah 5:2), *prince* (see Isaiah 9:6; Ezekiel 34:24; 37:25), *shepherd* (see Ezekiel 34:23; 37:24; Micah 5:4; Zechariah 13:7), *servant* (see Psalm 89:3, 20; Isaiah 42:1; 50:10; 52:13; 53:11; Jeremiah 33:21, 22, 26; Ezekiel 34:23-24; 37:24-25; Zechariah 3:8), and *dominion* (see Psalm 72:8, KJV; Daniel 7:14). (4) Finally, there are words describing his (s)election by God, such as *called* (see Isaiah 42:6; 49:1), *chosen* (see Psalm 89:3; Isaiah 42:1; 49:7), *anointed* (see 1 Samuel 2:10; Psalm 18:50; 45:7; 89:20; 132:17; Isaiah 61:1; Daniel 9:25; Habakkuk 3:13), and *covenant* (see Psalm 89:3, 28; 132:12; Isaiah 42:6; 49:8; 59:21; Jeremiah 31:31-34; 33:20-21; Ezekiel 37:26; Malachi 3:1).

2. Some of the vocabulary is quite violent: *conquer* (see Numbers 24:17-19), *crush* (see Habakkuk 3:13), *destroy* (see Isaiah 11:13), *wrath* and *perish* (see Psalm 2:12, KJV), and *enemies* (see Psalm 110:1-4; 132:18). One of the Dead Sea Scrolls states, "He shall crush the temples of Moab, and cut to pieces all the sons of Sheth" (4Q175). This is not so different than Revelation 19:11-21, where Jesus is depicted as returning on a warhorse with a garment stained with his enemies' blood.
3. For more on this, see Kenneth Atkinson, "The Militant Davidic Messiah and Violence Against Rome: The Influence of Pompey on the Development of Jewish and Christian Messianism" *Scripta Judaica Cracoviensia* 9 (February 2012): 7–19, https://doi.org/10.4467/20843925SJ.11.001.0159.
4. The only prophet who was known to be anointed was Elisha, although Psalm 105:15 implies that prophetic anointing was common: "Do not touch my anointed ones; do my prophets no harm."
5. Zechariah 6:12-13 and Malachi 3:1-4 also talk about the priestly role of the Messiah. This is reflected in the Dead Sea Scrolls, which talk about a Messiah with the dual role of king and priest without addressing the contradiction of a kingly priest (1QS IX, 11–12 and 1QSa II, 11–22; see also *Jubilees* 31:12-17, *Testament of Dan* 5:10, and *Testament of Judah* 21:2-5). 11Q13, however, leans into the image of Melchizedek in the same way Psalm 110:4 and Hebrews 5:6-10 do, thus solving the conundrum of a kingly priest.

CHAPTER 3: THE CHRIST CAPTCHA

1. Isaiah 61 was cited in the Qumran scrolls (11Q13, called 11QMelchizedek), the *Targum Jonathan* on Isaiah 61, the Babylonian Talmud (*b. Megillah* 23b), and the Midrash Rabbah of Leviticus 10:1 and Lamentations 3:60.
2. There's more here than meets the eye. Jesus was not the first to add the idea of resurrection to this very passage. The Qumran community had a scroll (4Q521) that combined these same two texts (Isaiah 35 and 61). Furthermore, they added the same phrase Jesus did: "He will raise the dead." That's too much similarity to be a coincidence. Jesus, combining Isaiah 35 and 61 and adding the idea of resurrection, is likely referencing Qumran rather than creating something new. At the very least, Jesus was familiar with an idea the Essenes cherished: that the hope for a Messiah was more than people imagined. This subtle clue could have been Jesus' way of saying, "John, I see you. I know where you are and what you're going through. Don't lose heart, for I will be more than you hoped." This is a message we should all be attuned to hear.

CHAPTER 4: MORPHING THE MESSIAH

1. See Hosea 3:5; Amos 9:11-15; Habakkuk 3:13; *1 Enoch* 52:4-9; *Jubilees* 31:12-20; *Targum Pseudo-Jonathan* on Genesis 49:11; *Targum Isaiah* 10:27; 4Q285; Philo, *Rewards and Punishments* 16.91-97.

2. To understand how Jewish writers grappled with this trauma, see particularly Songs 2 and 8 in the *Psalms of Solomon*. Joel Willitts, "Matthew and Psalms of Solomon's Messianism: A Comparative Study in First-Century Messianology," *Bulletin for Biblical Research* 22, no. 1 (2012): 27–50, https://doi.org/10.2307/26424609.
3. *Psalm of Solomon* 17 expresses this longing for David's heir to make things right. The writings from Qumran tell the same story—every reference to the "Branch of David" in those texts comes from this period under Herod. They wanted Herod gone and the new David installed.
4. I. J. du Plessis, "The Relation Between the Old and the New Testaments from the Perspective of Kingship/Kingdom—Including the Messianic Motif," *Neotestamentica* 14 (1980): 52, https://www.jstor.org/stable/43047806.
5. According to Josephus, it was "an ambiguous oracle . . . '[that] about that time, one from their country should become governor of the habitable earth'" (*Wars of the Jews*, 6.312). This prophecy—likely from the book of Daniel—reflects how intense messianic expectations had become.
6. John Mark Jones, "Subverting the Textuality of Davidic Messianism: Matthew's Presentation of the Genealogy and the Davidic Title," *The Catholic Biblical Quarterly* 56, no. 2 (1994): 256–272, https://www.jstor.org/stable/43721631.
7. Here is an excerpt from Justin Martyr illustrating this style: "The Word of God is His Son. . . . [And He,] being the first-begotten Word of God, is even God. And of old He appeared in the shape of fire and in the likeness of an angel to Moses and to the other prophets; but now in the times of your reign, having, as we before said, become Man by a virgin." From Justin Martyr, "The First Apology," in *The Ante-Nicene Fathers*, edited by Alexander Roberts and James Donaldson, vol. 1, 187 (Buffalo, 1886).

CHAPTER 5: WHEN JESUS GOT WEIRD

1. Luca von Burkersroda, "20 Bizzare TikTok Trends That Are Taking Over 2025," Festivaltopia, May 13, 2025, https://festivaltopia.com/20-bizarre-tiktok-trends-that-are-taking-over-2025/.
2. Joseph Henrich et al., "The Weirdest People in the World?" *Behavioral and Brain Sciences* 33, no. 2 (2010): 61–83, https://doi.org/10.1017/s0140525x0999152x.
3. Robert D. Putnam, *Bowling Alone: The Collapse and Revival of American Community* (Simon & Schuster, 2000).
4. Christian Smith with Melinda Lundquist Denton, *Soul Searching: The Religious and Spiritual Lives of American Teenagers* (Oxford University Press, 2005).
5. Byung-Chul Han, *The Burnout Society* (Stanford University Press, 2015), 9.
6. Richard B. Hays, *The Moral Vision of the New Testament: Community, Cross, New Creation; A Contemporary Introduction to New Testament Ethics* (HarperSanFrancisco, 1996), 9.

CHAPTER 6: THE MESSIAH THEY PREDICTED

1. A descendant of David (see 2 Samuel 7:12-16; Matthew 1:1; Romans 1:3), born in Bethlehem (see Micah 5:2; Matthew 2:1), to a virgin (see Isaiah 7:14; Matthew 1:18-23; Luke 1:26-35). A miracle worker (see Isaiah 35:5-6; 61:1; Matthew 11:4-5; John 20:30-31) and a light to the Gentiles (see Isaiah 42:6; 49:6; Luke 2:32; Acts 13:47). A suffering servant (see Isaiah 53:3-12; Psalm 22; Matthew 27:27-50; 1 Peter 2:24), rejected by his own people (see Isaiah 53:3; Psalm 118:22; John 1:11; 1 Peter 2:7), betrayed for thirty pieces of silver (see Zechariah 11:12-13; Matthew 26:15), and crucified (see Psalm 22:16; Zechariah 12:10; John 19:18). Raised from the dead (see Psalm 16:10; Isaiah 53:10-11; 1 Corinthians 15:3-4) and ascended to God's right hand (see Psalm 110:1; Acts 1:9). A priest and king like Melchizedek (see Psalm 110:4; Hebrews 6:20) and an arbiter of the new covenant (see Jeremiah 31:31-34; Luke 22:20).
2. Several other passages also talk about Israel as God's child (see Isaiah 43:6; Jeremiah 31:9; Hosea 1:10).
3. Though the Gentile converts would have a model of Son of God in their emperors, Jews did not have such an easy linkage to the Messiah. There is, however, an "Easter Egg" in the story of King David. When God established David's dynasty, he declared, "I will be his father, and he will be my son. When he does wrong, I will punish him with a rod wielded by men, with floggings inflicted by human hands" (2 Samuel 7:14). It wasn't that David and his descendants were divine; it was that they represented the nation. That's how this title got attached to the Messiah. Both Psalm 2:7 and Psalm 89:26-27 promise a Messiah, chosen by God, who would rescue and represent the nation. Here's the bottom line: King David became the linkage for the future Messiah as God's Son.

CHAPTER 7: THE MESSIAH NO ONE SAW COMING, PART 1

1. Craig A. Evans, "Predictions of the Destruction of the Herodian Temple in the Pseudepigrapha, Qumran Scrolls, and Related Texts," *JSP* 5, no. 10 (1992): 89–147, https://doi.org/10.1177/095182079200001008; Jesus was not the first or last to critique the Temple. Jeremiah did it six hundred years earlier, and they threatened to kill him for it (Jeremiah 26:1-19). Sabbeus and Theodosius were killed for supporting a rival temple in Egypt (Josephus, *Antiquities*, 13.79). Among the Essenes, an attempt was made on the life of the "Teacher of Righteousness" for his criticism of the Temple (1 QpHab XI, 4–8; cf. 1 QpHab IX, 9f; 4QPs 37 4, 8f). And Jesus, son of Ananias, was dragged before the Roman procurator for his prophecy against the Temple (Josephus, *Jewish War*, 6.300–305).

2. Colin Brown, ed., *The New International Dictionary of New Testament Theology*, vol. 3 (Zondervan, 1978), 781.

CHAPTER 8: THE MESSIAH NO ONE SAW COMING, PART 2

1. Maarten J. J. Menken, "The Textual Form and Meaning of the Quotation from Zechariah 12:10 in John 19:37," *The Catholic Biblical Quarterly* 55, no. 3 (1993): 494–511. The Hebrew verb דָּקַר (*daqar*, "pierced") was rendered in the Septuagint with the word "danced" (*κατορχέομαι*), reflecting the theological struggle with God suffering or being pierced.
2. Alexander Sperber, ed., *The Bible in Aramaic: Based on Old Manuscripts and Printed Texts*, vol. 3, *The Latter Prophets* (E. J. Brill, 1962).
3. Craig A. Evans, *Jesus and His Contemporaries: Comparative Studies* (E. J. Brill, 2001), 381–406; "Psalm 118:22," Intertextual.bible, accessed November 11, 2025, https://intertextual.bible/text/psalm-118.22-targum-psalm-118.22-matthew-21.42.
4. C. S. Lewis, *Mere Christianity* (HarperOne, 2001), 205.
5. See Targum Jonathan to Isaiah 9:6 in Alexander Sperber, ed., *The Bible in Aramaic: Based on Old Manuscripts and Printed Texts*, vol. 3, *The Latter Prophets* (E. J. Brill, 1962); William G. Braude, ed., *Pesikta Rabbati: Discourses for Feasts, Fasts, and Special Sabbaths*, vol. 1 (Yale University Press, 1968), 36.

CHAPTER 9: THE COMEBACK THAT PROVED HIS MESSIAHSHIP

1. In addition to the Old Testament texts that indicate his eternal rule, 2 Baruch 40:1-2 says, "The last leader of that time will be left alive . . . and My Messiah will convict him of all his impieties. . . . And his principate will stand for ever." First Maccabees 2:57 says, "David, because he was merciful, inherited the throne of the kingdom forever," and 4Q246 says, "He will be called son of God, and they will call him son of the Most High . . . His kingdom will be an eternal kingdom, and all his paths in truth."

CHAPTER 10: FROM FAN TO FOLLOWER

1. My professor's name was Dr. Mark Moore, and it's interesting to be writing this chapter in this book, because thirty years ago, he was the one who helped teach this idea to me. He was the kind of professor who would dock points if your bibliography wasn't formatted in perfect Turabian style and who insisted that margins be exactly 1 inch, not 1.1 inches, not 0.9 inches, but exactly 1 inch. I'm still a little bitter for getting a B+ on a paper about grace because I had "inconsistent" footnotes. But despite his slightly obsessive attention to academic detail, he understood something profound: The goal of studying Jesus isn't to master information about him but to be mastered by him.

2. Dallas Willard, *The Divine Conspiracy: Discovering Our Hidden Life in God* (HarperSanFrancisco, 1998), 41.

AFTERWORD: BETWEEN THE BANQUETS

1. "Seven Signs Pointing to Jesus as the Messiah," accessed November 24, 2025, https://www.esv.org/resources/esv-global-study-bible/chart-43-03/.

ABOUT THE AUTHORS

KYLE IDLEMAN is a bestselling author and the senior pastor at Southeast Christian Church in Louisville, Kentucky, one of the largest churches in America. Kyle is the author of *Not a Fan*, *One at a Time*, *The End of Me*, *Gods at War*, *Grace Is Greater*, and *Don't Give Up*. Kyle's favorite thing to do is to hang out with the love of his life, DesiRae. They have four children: MacKenzie, Morgan, Macy, and Kael.

MARK E. MOORE is the bestselling author of *Core 52* and the teaching pastor at Christ's Church of the Valley in Peoria, Arizona, one of the fastest growing and most dynamic churches in America. He previously spent two decades as a New Testament professor at Ozark Christian College. His life's passion is to make Scripture accessible and relevant to people trying to make sense of Christianity. Mark and his wife, Barbara, live in Peoria.